Empowering Students

Transitioning From Management to Accountability

Brad Johnson

Empowering Students

Published by TeacherGoals Publishing, LLC, Beech Grove, IN
www.teachergoals.com
Cover Design by: Tricia Fuglestad
Interior Design by: Aubrey Labitigan
Edited by: Carrie Turner
Copy Edited by: Jennifer Bindus

Library of Congress Control Number: 2024940563
Paperback ISBN: 978-1-959419-25-9
ASIN: B0D55K7KPF
First Printing July 2024

TEACHERGOALS
PUBLISHING

Dedication

To the dedicated teachers who go above and beyond to build strong connections with their students, creating classrooms where every child feels seen and valued. Your hard work and passion make a world of difference. This book is for you, in appreciation of the incredible impact you have on your students' lives. Keep inspiring and empowering the next generation. You are the difference makers!

Reviews

"If you're looking for a great book about education written by someone who's actively in the trenches, this is the book for you. I deeply appreciate Brad's perspective because he's genuinely engaged in the schools, and it's evident in every chapter of this book. If you're aiming to be the best you can be, this book is for you. Brad brings his insights and professional experiences to life, sharing them with us to improve as educators, administrators, and professionals in any educational role. I highly recommend this book to anyone dedicated to excelling in their role as an educator."

-Gerry Brooks, Elementary School Principal and Author of *Go See the Principal*

"There were several instances during the review when I found myself physically shaking my head in agreement with all statements. Brad had me at the statement, 'Classroom management is undeniably one of the most critical aspects of teaching.'

I appreciated the topics Brad provided (Assertive Teaching, Relationships, Pygmalion Effect, Empowering Classrooms, etc...), explanations for the importance of each subject, and the strategies to help instructional leaders address the never-ending challenges that present themselves each year in education.

Teachers deal with the most precious resource for our future, and they need practical support to help create more opportunities for improving their experiences in teaching and learning and growing our kids daily. Thank you, Brad, for sharing this book, and I look forward to using your information in the future to aid in developing our educators."

-Kelly D. Grondahl, Vegas Verdes Elementary School Principal

"Empowering Students is a must-read for educators seeking practical, transformative strategies to use in their classrooms. Dr. Johnson expertly navigates the complexities of modern teaching, providing actionable insights on creating positive classroom environments and enhancing teacher assertiveness. His emphasis on empowering students for lasting change is both timely and impactful, offering a refreshing shift from traditional behavior management approaches. Dr. Johnson's passion for education shines through, inspiring educators to cultivate accountability and foster meaningful student growth.

-Dr. Rachel Edoho-Eket, Author of *The Principal's Journey*

Contents

Introduction

Classroom management is undeniably one of the most critical aspects of teaching. It makes the difference between a smooth, energizing day and a chaotic, exhausting experience. Effective management not only reduces disruptions but also creates a positive learning environment. This, in turn, makes teaching more fulfilling for educators.

Consider this: a well-managed classroom means less time spent on behavior issues and more time devoted to teaching. It means engaging with your students and delivering quality lessons. The result is a sense of accomplishment and fulfillment at the end of the day.

During Covid, I shared the following quote on social media to encourage educators.

"Relationships before rigor. Grace before grades. Patience before programs. Love before lessons."

That quote ended up resonating within the education community in unexpected ways because other educators understood what it means. The quote encapsulates what I believe is the essence of effective teaching. It emphasizes the importance of seeing students as individuals first and foremost, which highlights the significance of building meaningful relationships in the learning process. It's crucial to see students not just as learners in the classroom but also to recognize their potential beyond academic achievements. We must nurture that.

The key is for teachers to move away from the role of disciplinarians and into the role of leaders who empower students to take responsibility for their behavior. Educational experts like Dr. Linda Albert and Dr. William Glasser emphasize the importance of student accountability in classroom management. By fostering a culture of respect and self-discipline, teachers not only reduce their workload but also nurture independence and maturity in their students.

Moreover, effective classroom management creates a positive feedback loop. When students experience a structured and supportive environment, they become more motivated and engaged, resulting in improved academic performance. Motivated, successful students boost teachers' confidence levels and their passion for education, creating a cycle of success and growth.

While traditional methods focus on rules and consequences, the real magic lies in nurturing resilience and igniting a passion for exploration. By tapping into students' strengths and passions, educators can unlock their full potential and create dynamic, engaging learning experiences. This approach shifts the focus from behavior management to active participation and collaboration, benefiting both students and teachers alike.

In the following chapters, we'll examine actionable strategies rooted in empathy, understanding, and student accountability. It will include concepts like the Pygmalion Effect, Educere, and divergent learning, which are all designed to transform disruptions into opportunities for change. By implementing these strategies, educators can create classroom environments where students thrive, take ownership of their learning, and become active partners in their educational journey.

1

Assertive Teaching: Transforming Classrooms for Impact

While every teacher aspires to be effective, I know one educator who took it to a whole different level. Her name was Tammy McElory and she was—hands down—the best teacher I've ever seen. I had the fortune of teaching with her for several years, and she was an inspiration to me. Years later, when I moved into administration, I still relied on her experience and expertise. What set Tammy apart was her exceptional ability to balance assertiveness, personalized connections, and a hands-on approach to real-world learning.

Tammy's exceptional teaching style seamlessly blended assertive traits with personalized approaches, creating a classroom environment that nurtured each student's unique needs. By setting clear expectations, establishing boundaries between school and home life, and handling conflicts with confidence, Tammy ensured positive outcomes and a conducive learning atmosphere. Her instinctive leadership and rejection of a one-size-fits-all approach revealed her dedication to student success and well-being.

For instance, if Tammy had a student who was having difficulties cooperating with their partner during a classroom activity, she might facilitate a conversation between the two students, emphasizing the importance of finding common ground and respecting each other's contributions. She would focus on their strengths and how they could contribute effectively. They would be encouraged to leverage their unique skills to benefit the team's overall success. Likewise, if a student struggled and wanted to work alone, she may accommodate them. Simply put, she knew what each student needed and would adapt to make it work.

She also made learning enjoyable and relevant to the real world, which was a refreshing departure from traditional textbook methods. I remember one time she introduced a unique game for adults entering her classroom. To gain entry, they had to answer questions related to the day's lesson, a small yet effective strategy. The positive response from her students showed the success of this approach. It also made adults think twice before interrupting her class.

Tammy excelled at building relationships, ensuring that every student felt seen and understood. Even students who struggled in other classes enjoyed her class because they felt she genuinely understood their needs and really cared. Her classroom wasn't just about imparting information; it was a dynamic environment that catered to diverse student needs and fostered a sense of belonging.

The magic happened in Tammy's ability to weave these elements together seamlessly. Her assertiveness provided structure without stifling individuality. Students knew the boundaries, yet they felt free to express themselves. It was this unique balance that kept her classroom running smoothly. And I remember her motto, which is almost cliché anymore, but she meant it when she said, "If we work hard, we play hard."

As I reflect on all my years in education, Tammy McElroy's

impact is not just a memory but a benchmark for effective teaching. The secret to her success, and a valuable takeaway for the reader of this book, lies in her expert balance between building relationships and being assertive. Here's to thirty years of practical wisdom, and a salute to the unparalleled mastery of Tammy McElroy! Having discussed the inspiring journey of an exceptional educator, let's explore a deeper understanding of assertiveness.

Understanding Assertiveness: The Cornerstone of Effective Teaching

As an educator, you've likely encountered the common misconception that assertiveness is synonymous with aggression. It's crucial to debunk these misconceptions as we delve into the critical role of assertiveness in effective teaching.

Assertiveness is not aggression; it's a communication style that empowers you to confidently convey your thoughts, needs, and expectations. It requires a deliberate approach, striking a balance between firmness and respect. Assertiveness is about expressing yourself clearly while embracing diverse perspectives and fostering understanding.

Like any other skill set, assertiveness can be developed with practice. It involves learning to stand up for yourself without being either aggressive or passive. This skill set is beneficial for individuals with either low or high agreeableness, as they can work on developing and enhancing their assertiveness skills through self-reflection and intentional changes in behavior.

As a teacher, being assertive offers you multiple benefits. It can allow you to effectively manage your classroom, communicate with students, balance authority with empathy, collaborate with colleagues and parents, manage stress, and promote your professional growth.

Maintaining a balance between your authority as an educator and empathy for your students allows you to create a supportive and respectful classroom atmosphere. Assertiveness also facilitates effective collaboration with your colleagues and parents, leading to productive partnerships and better outcomes for everyone. It also equips you with the skills to manage stress and maintain a healthy work-life balance by expressing your needs and setting boundaries.

By advocating for yourself, seeking professional development opportunities, and confidently expressing your ideas and opinions, you can foster your own professional growth and advancement. In essence, assertiveness is a critical skill for educators that shapes positive teacher-student dynamics and contributes to a positive school culture.

Now that we understand the essence of assertiveness, let's explore practical strategies for cultivating assertiveness skills in educators. Developing assertiveness as an educator involves understanding your communication style and its impact on classroom dynamics. It's essential to recognize that assertiveness is not about being confrontational or dominating. Rather, it's about communicating expectations, setting boundaries, and fostering a collaborative learning environment.

Assertive communication involves not only expressing yourself clearly but also listening to others' perspectives and showing empathy. This helps build trust and mutual respect in the classroom and among colleagues.

Setting clear expectations and boundaries is also key to assertiveness. Communicate your expectations to students regarding behavior, assignments, and classroom rules. Consistency in enforcing these expectations helps establish a structured learning environment and reduces misunderstandings.

Additionally, practicing assertiveness in difficult situations can be challenging but rewarding. When addressing conflicts or addressing challenging behaviors, it's crucial to stay calm, using assertive language, and focusing on finding solutions rather than blaming or criticizing.

Lastly, seek feedback from colleagues, mentors, or professional development resources to continually improve your assertiveness skills. Reflect on your communication style, identify areas for growth, and take proactive steps to enhance your skill.

By incorporating these practical strategies and embracing assertiveness as a crucial skill, you'll not only enhance your effectiveness as an educator but also create a positive and empowering learning environment for your students. Being assertive as a teacher also lays the groundwork for assertiveness in schools.

The Need for Assertiveness

As you embark on your teaching journey, it's important to recognize that teachers often exhibit a personality trait known as high agreeableness. These qualities of agreeableness include compassion, empathy, kindness, and care, which are traits you want in a teacher. It is also characterized by a tendency to prioritize harmony, avoid conflict, and be overly accommodating, which can impact your ability to be assertive in the classroom. Understanding and addressing this tendency is crucial for developing effective assertiveness skills, especially where your students are concerned.

Highly agreeable teachers may find it challenging to navigate situations that require assertiveness, because it can feel uncomfortable at first. The reluctance to engage in conflict can lead to difficulties in managing disruptive behavior, setting clear boundaries, and effectively communicating expectations. Without assertiveness, maintaining a structured and positive learning environment becomes increasingly complex.

Moreover, the accommodating nature of high agreeableness can blur boundaries and result in inconsistency in disciplinary actions. This lack of clarity can hinder your ability to manage classroom dynamics and create a conducive learning environment for your students.

To overcome these challenges, you can benefit from developing assertiveness skills tailored to your personality traits. This involves learning to express your thoughts, needs, and expectations confidently and respectfully. By practicing assertive communication, you can establish clear boundaries, address conflicts constructively, and foster a positive and structured learning environment that supports student growth and success.

Additionally, cultivating assertiveness empowers you to balance empathy and authority effectively. It enables you to empathize with students' perspectives while maintaining control, so that you can guide them towards positive behavior. Assertive teachers also find it easier to collaborate with colleagues, engage parents in meaningful discussions, and advocate for their professional development needs.

In summary, recognizing the impact of high agreeableness on assertiveness is essential for educators like you to enhance communication, leadership, and classroom management skills. By acknowledging and addressing this trait, you can cultivate assertiveness, improve classroom dynamics, and create a more supportive and productive learning environment that benefits everyone. As you develop assertiveness, the impact will be felt not only in your classroom, but throughout your school and community.

The Ripple Effect: The Impact of Assertiveness on Classroom and Beyond

When you integrate assertiveness into your teaching methodology, there's a profound shift. It marks the beginning of a transformative journey. This approach empowers you to set clear boundaries and expectations upfront, creating a structured learning environment that reduces confusion and nurtures a sense of accountability among your students. For example, implementing a detailed classroom code of conduct with defined behaviors and consequences highlights your commitment to maintaining order and fostering responsibility.

Assertiveness goes beyond disciplinary measures. It becomes a cornerstone for resolving conflicts effectively and fostering critical life skills among students. As an educator who prioritizes constructive conflict resolution, you showcase the importance of respectful dialogue and problem-solving. This not only resolves immediate issues but also equips students with valuable skills applicable in various real-life scenarios, enhancing their overall personal development.

The impact isn't confined to the classroom alone; it extends its influence on the broader educational landscape, shaping the collective impact teachers have beyond their individual classrooms. This proactive mindset fosters a culture of respect, accountability, and collaboration not only among students but also among fellow educators and the school community. This ripple effect translates into a more positive and conducive learning environment across the entire educational institution.

Assertiveness isn't solely about managing behavior or addressing conflicts. It's about nurturing a culture of respect and responsibility. As an educator who embodies proactive communication, you shape positive communication patterns among students. They learn to express themselves confidently and respectfully, fostering healthier interactions and stronger relationships within the school environment.

Additionally, this approach serves as an effective strategy against prevalent issues like bullying. By implementing a zero-tolerance policy for bullying and promptly addressing such behaviors consistently, you send a clear message that bullying is unacceptable, fostering a safer and more inclusive environment for all students.

This mindset significantly contributes to shaping the broader school culture. As an educator who embodies a proactive stance, you become a role model for respectful communication and conflict resolution, cultivating a culture of empathy, cooperation, and mutual respect that transcends individual classrooms and positively influences the entire school community.

The benefits of embracing an assertive approach extend to you as a teacher as well. It empowers you to manage your classroom effectively, navigate challenging situations with confidence, and enhance communication with colleagues and parents. Embracing this proactive stance also enables you to advocate for your needs and those of your students, fostering a collaborative and supportive educational environment.

To fully harness the potential, continuous professional development focused on proactive communication, conflict resolution, and creating a positive classroom culture is essential. Engaging in workshops, seminars, and peer mentoring programs equips you with practical strategies and tools to further enhance your skills, creating an even more engaging and supportive learning environment.

In essence, an assertive mindset isn't just a teaching technique. Rather, it's a guiding philosophy that has the power to transform your classroom and educational experiences holistically. By embracing this proactive approach, you cultivate a structured, respectful, and empowering learning environment that benefits everyone, leading to enhanced academic success as well as personal growth. Now, let's examine ten strategies to help you cultivate this powerful approach.

Cultivating Assertiveness and Effective Teaching Skills for an Impactful Classroom

Creating a positive and productive learning environment for students is vital, and assertiveness plays a crucial role in your success. Assertive teachers can establish authority, maintain discipline, and build healthy relationships with students. They effectively communicate expectations, address conflicts, and handle challenging situations with confidence. In the next section, we will explore ten strategies that can help you become more assertive and cultivate effective teaching skills, ultimately creating the positive classroom environment you want.

Ten Strategies for Assertive Teaching and Positive Classroom Culture

1. Setting Clear Boundaries and Expectations

As an educator, setting clear boundaries and expectations is paramount to creating a structured and conducive learning environment. You should communicate rules and consequences explicitly to help students understand the guidelines and their importance in maintaining a safe and respectful classroom atmosphere. Providing specific examples of rules and consequences, along with explanations, will reinforce the rationale behind these guidelines, promoting student ownership and comprehension.

Additionally, setting boundaries with workload distribution and commitments helps you avoid taking on more than you can handle. By prioritizing tasks and delegating when necessary, you can prevent feeling overwhelmed and exhausted, contributing to your long-term well-being and job satisfaction.

2. Emphasizing Consistency

Consistency is key in promoting fairness and building trust among your students. You should maintain consistency in expectations and consequences to ensure your students understand what is expected of them consistently, leading to a more predictable and reliable learning environment. Consistent feedback and grading practices also play a crucial role in motivating your students and enhancing their performance by providing clear and timely guidance on their progress.

3. Effective Communication Techniques

Utilizing effective communication techniques such as "I" statements and active listening enhances your interactions with students and colleagues. "I" statements help diffuse conflicts by focusing on your personal experiences and feelings rather than blame, promoting open dialogue and problem-solving. Active listening, on the other hand, builds relationships and cultivates a supportive classroom culture by demonstrating empathy and understanding. Emphasizing these communication strategies encourages positive interactions and meaningful connections within the educational community.

4. Building Self-Confidence

Encouraging yourself to focus on your strengths and seek professional development opportunities is essential for building self-confidence. Identifying and leveraging your personal strengths in teaching practices not only enhances your confidence but also improves your teaching effectiveness and student engagement.

Ongoing professional development plays a crucial role in expanding your skills, addressing challenges, and adapting your teaching approaches to meet the diverse needs of students, ultimately boosting your confidence and competence.

5. Developing Problem-Solving Skills

Empowering students through problem-solving processes and collaboration fosters teamwork. Encouraging student involvement in problem-solving activities promotes active learning and deeper understanding of concepts. Providing examples of real-world problems or scenarios where students can apply problem-solving strategies enhances their skills and prepares them for future challenges.

6. Practicing Positive Self-Talk

Teaching yourself the practice of replacing negative self-talk with affirmations is instrumental in boosting your self-confidence and resiliency. Offering specific techniques for reframing negative thoughts into positive affirmations equips you with valuable tools for maintaining a positive mindset and overcoming challenges. Emphasizing the impact of positive self-talk on mindset, resiliency, and overall well-being encourages a supportive and optimistic learning environment.

7. Seeking Support and Feedback

Engaging with colleagues and mentors for insights and feedback is a valuable strategy for your continuous improvement. Collaborating with peers and mentors allows you to gain new perspectives, refine your teaching practices, and address areas for growth. Actively seeking feedback and implementing suggestions for professional development contributes to your ongoing learning and enhances your effectiveness.

8. Cultivating Self-Compassion

Embracing your own imperfections and practicing self-compassion promotes your personal growth and well-being. It also teaches students how to embrace self-compassion in their own lives. Discussing the concept of self-compassion and its role in fostering resilience and self-care is essential for maintaining a healthy work-life balance. Strategies such as mindfulness, self-reflection, and setting realistic expectations helps you prioritize self-care and sustain your energy and enthusiasm in the classroom.

9. Focusing on Strengths

Celebrating and showcasing your strengths enhances your personal confidence. When you celebrate your students' strengths, it promotes engagement and learning outcomes in your class. Encouraging yourself to integrate your strengths into lesson design, instructional methods, and student interactions creates a more personalized and effective learning experience. Sharing success stories or examples of leveraging strengths inspires you to capitalize on your unique abilities and create meaningful connections with students.

10. Practicing Self-Care

Prioritizing your well-being and self-care is essential for you to bring your best self to the classroom. Providing yourself with a comprehensive self-care plan that includes strategies for physical health, mental well-being, and work-life balance supports you in sustaining energy, enthusiasm, and effectiveness. The importance of practicing self-care is clear. It fosters a positive teaching environment that benefits you as well as your students.

Cultivating assertiveness and effective teaching skills is fundamental to creating a positive classroom environment. By implementing the ten strategies outlined above, you can empower yourself to set clear boundaries, communicate effectively, foster collaboration, and prioritize self-care. Assertive teaching not only benefits you but also enhances the overall learning experience for your students, leading to improved outcomes and a more fulfilling educational journey.

Assertiveness with Non-Conforming Students

Assertiveness becomes particularly crucial when dealing with non-conforming students. These students may challenge traditional norms, question authority, or exhibit behavior that deviates from conventional expectations. Understanding and practicing assertiveness is an indispensable tool for educators in effective classroom management.

Non-conforming students often test boundaries, seeking autonomy and individual expression. In such situations, assertiveness serves to establish clear expectations without resorting to aggression. By confidently communicating boundaries, you can create an environment where non-conforming students understand the limits while still feeling respected and heard.

It's important to recognize that assertiveness, in this context, is not about stifling individuality but rather about providing a framework for constructive expression. Non-conforming students often exhibit low agreeableness traits such as:

1. **Questioning Authority:** Non-conforming students may challenge traditional authority structures and seek to understand the rationale behind rules and decisions. This can lead to conflicts or disruptions in the classroom.

2. **Autonomy Seeking:** They value independence, preferring to make their own choices and decisions whenever possible. This desire for autonomy can sometimes clash with classroom rules and expectations.

3. **Individual Expression:** Non-conforming students often express themselves uniquely through unconventional ideas

or non-traditional approaches to learning. This can be positive. However, it may also create challenges to classroom structure.

4. **Boundary Testing:** They may explore and push limits to prove their individuality, which can manifest as behavior that challenges classroom norms. This boundary testing behavior can disrupt class dynamics. This may require clear and assertive management strategies.

By acknowledging and addressing these traits with assertive communication and management techniques, you as an educator can effectively navigate challenges posed by non-conforming students. Navigating this effectively will create a positive and inclusive learning environment for all students.

Moreover, assertiveness will help you address behavioral challenges with a nuanced approach. Instead of reacting impulsively, you can be the assertive teacher who engages non-conforming students in open dialogue, encouraging them to express their thoughts and concerns. This intentional communication not only defuses potential conflicts but also empowers students to voice their opinions within the boundaries of a structured, respectful learning environment.

The application of assertiveness with non-conforming students goes beyond managing behavior; it becomes a tool for mentorship and guidance. By actively listening to the concerns and ideas of non-conforming students, educators can identify opportunities for personalized support and mentorship, aiding in their academic and personal development.

In essence, assertiveness is a vital skill for navigating the complexities of the classroom, especially when faced with non-conforming students. When wielded effectively, assertiveness empowers educators to maintain control, establish clear expectations, and create an inclusive environment that encourages every student to contribute to their learning community and ultimately thrive regardless of conformity. By embracing assertiveness in the face of non-conformity, you can uphold the principles of effective teaching but also contribute to the broader goal of nurturing confident critical thinkers.

Teaching with Impact: The Assertiveness Advantage

Assertiveness isn't just a skill; it's a superpower for educators. Maybe that's why I always thought of my friend Tammy as a superhero! It empowers teachers to create a positive, structured, and respectful classroom environment conducive to effective teaching and learning. An assertive teacher excels at classroom management due to several key factors:

Firstly, clear communication is paramount. Assertive teachers communicate expectations, rules, and consequences clearly and consistently. This reduces confusion and misunderstandings among students, because such transparency ensures that students understand what is expected of them. In other words, it promotes accountability.

Secondly, assertiveness is a superpower because it helps teachers enforce discipline respectfully, addressing misbehavior promptly without hostility or aggression. This fosters mutual respect and maintains a positive classroom atmosphere where students feel safe and supported in their learning journey.

Confidence plays a crucial role as well. Assertive teachers exude confidence, which has a calming effect on the classroom and encourages students to follow instructions and behave appropriately while modeling calm confidence themselves. This confidence also inspires trust and credibility in the teacher-student relationship.

Active listening is another hallmark of assertive teaching.

Teachers who actively listen to students' concerns and feedback demonstrate value for their opinions, promoting a sense of belonging and positive engagement. This fosters a collaborative learning environment where students feel heard and understood.

Lastly, boundary setting is key. Assertive teachers establish and maintain clear boundaries regarding behavior, academic standards, and classroom activities. This creates a structured learning environment where students feel secure and understand acceptable behavior, leading to a more focused, productive classroom.

Although assertive teaching is not solely about managing behavior, it plays a crucial role in creating a learning environment where students feel safe, which frees them to become their best selves. This combination of assertive teaching strategies creates a transformative educational experience where every student can reach their full potential and—to put it simply—thrive.

2

Building Positive Relationships: Fostering Connection in the Classroom

In the busy halls of the middle school where I taught, there was a student we'll call Jake. He always sat quietly at the back of the class, not causing any disruptions but appearing somewhat distant. Over time, I noticed a change in Jake; he seemed sadder and more disconnected. Feeling concerned, I decided to talk to him one day after class.

"Hey, Jake," I said. "Is everything alright?"

It took a moment, but eventually, he opened up about his parents' divorce, which was affecting him deeply. I wanted to help.

Knowing Jake's passion for video games, I organized a game night at the school and invited students, parents, and chaperones to participate. It turned out Jake was a skilled gamer, and by the end of the evening, everyone wanted him to be on their team. This event transformed Jake's demeanor, and when he returned to class on

Monday, he seemed like a different person, someone more talkative and engaged in class. Perhaps most importantly, he was smiling. The game night was not just about gaming; it was a way to connect with Jake and show him that I cared.

As days passed, Jake started interacting more with other students, discussing video games, sharing strategies, and forming friendships within the classroom. This simple yet meaningful connection had a profound impact on him. His father later approached me, expressing gratitude for the positive change he observed in Jake after the game night.

Jake's story highlights the importance of building connections with students and recognizing the transformative power of connection in our students' lives. It exemplified the essence of "Relationships before rigor," emphasizing the significance of connection as the foundation for effective teaching.

As an educator, fostering positive relationships with your students is crucial for creating an inclusive and supportive learning environment. These connections not only promote active participation and academic success but also contribute to your students' sense of belonging and overall well-being. Effective communication, inclusive practices, and personalized attention all play vital roles in helping you build and sustain these positive relationships. These skills can give you the power to shape a thriving learning community where students flourish both academically and personally.

The impact of Jake's transformation extended far beyond the classroom, resonating with other students and fostering a more connected and supportive atmosphere school wide. This ripple effect showcased the profound influence that genuine care and connections can have on—not just a person—but an educational community.

The Importance of Building Positive Relationships in the Classroom

Building positive relationships in the classroom is the cornerstone of effective teaching, shaping an environment where students thrive emotionally, socially, and academically. As an educator, your impact goes beyond imparting knowledge; it's about fostering connections that ignite a passion for learning and inspire students to achieve their full potential.

When you authentically connect with your students, you validate their individuality and affirm their worth beyond academic performance. This validation creates a sense of belonging foundational to your students' holistic development and success both in and out of the classroom.

Creating a warm and inclusive classroom culture is paramount in cultivating these positive relationships. When students feel safe, respected, and valued, they are more engaged and collaborative. That's when they contribute happily to a vibrant learning community. Consistently demonstrating care and understanding towards each student builds trust and strengthens your teacher-student bond.

Effective communication is essential for sustaining positive relationships with your class. Actively listening to your students, providing meaningful feedback, and encouraging open dialogue will foster a culture of appreciation and understanding. This communication approach not only addresses your students' diverse needs but also reinforces their sense of significance and contribution to the learning process.

Embracing culturally responsive teaching practices further enriches these connections by honoring students' diverse backgrounds, experiences, and perspectives. By embracing diversity and celebrating individuality, you can create an inclusive classroom where every student feels seen, heard, and valued.

Prioritizing positive relationships in your classroom transforms the educational experience for everyone involved. It creates an empowering, collaborative environment where your students develop critical life skills such as empathy, communication, and resilience. Academic excellence will naturally flow from that. Investing in these meaningful connections is not just a professional obligation; it's a fulfilling journey that can enrich the lives of you and your students alike.

Strategies for Building Positive Relationships With Students

One of the foundational steps in cultivating positive relationships with students is to establish a welcoming and inclusive classroom environment. This begins by clearly defining behavioral expectations and creating a safe space where students feel free to express themselves without fear of judgment or discrimination. Educators can promote inclusivity by celebrating diversity, fostering acceptance, and promptly addressing any instances of bias or discrimination.

To foster a sense of belonging, teachers can incorporate activities that encourage students to share their interests, backgrounds, and experiences. This can be achieved through icebreaker games, group discussions, or simple activities like "show and tell." By encouraging students to express their individuality, educators convey the message that their voices and experiences are valued and respected.

Moreover, nurturing positive relationships with students is closely linked to minimizing the need for excessive rules and regulations. When students feel welcomed and valued within the classroom community, they are more likely to take responsibility for their behavior and contribute to a harmonious learning environment.

When students feel a genuine connection with their peers and educators, the necessity for numerous rules diminishes. It's similar to how explicit rules in public restrooms prohibiting certain behaviors become unnecessary when individuals feel a sense of ownership and respect for their environment. Personal ownership and responsibility based on connection changes things.

Building positive relationships goes beyond rule enforcement; it involves an awareness of the unique needs and backgrounds of each student. By acknowledging and appreciating diversity, educators contribute to an environment where every student feels accepted and valued. This forms the basis of positive relationships, enabling educators like you to navigate challenges and conflicts with understanding.

Furthermore, a classroom environment without overly restrictive rules allows for a more dynamic, engaging learning experience. Students are more likely to actively participate in discussions, express their thoughts openly, and take intellectual risks when they feel secure and supported.

Effective classroom management and positive relationships hinge on cultivating a welcoming atmosphere. By prioritizing inclusivity, celebrating diversity, and fostering a sense of belonging, educators not only create a positive learning environment but also reduce the reliance on rigid rules. That's when students naturally become active participants in maintaining a respectful classroom community.

Likewise, the use of non-verbal cues, such as maintaining eye contact, nodding in understanding, and employing facial expressions, can convey attentiveness and significantly enhance communication.

These cues play a crucial role in building rapport and creating a supportive environment where students feel heard and understood.

In addition to connecting with students, building relationships with parents and caregivers is equally important for a well-rounded educational approach. Involving families in the educational process provides educators with valuable insights into students' home environments, cultural backgrounds, and individual needs. Regular communication with parents through updates, newsletters, and parent-teacher conferences strengthens the partnership between educators and families. For instance, you could organize periodic meetings to discuss your students' progress, providing an opportunity for parents to share their perspectives and concerns. This collaborative approach ensures that students receive consistent support and encouragement both at home and in the classroom.

Building Positive Relationships Through Assertiveness

Building positive relationships through assertiveness involves using specific strategies. This can empower you to create a supportive, inclusive classroom environment where every student feels valued and supported.

For example, establishing clear boundaries and expectations can be achieved by setting ground rules at the beginning of the school year and consistently reinforcing them. This could include guidelines for respectful communication, participation in class activities, and consequences for inappropriate behavior. By communicating these expectations clearly (and early) while respecting your students' individuality, you can create a structured environment where everyone knows what is expected of them.

Practicing active empathy involves actively listening to students' concerns, acknowledging their emotions, and seeking to understand their viewpoints. For instance, during a classroom discussion, you can encourage students to share their thoughts and actively listen to each other without judgment. This creates a safe and supportive space where everyone feels heard and valued, enhancing trust and communication within the classroom.

Giving constructive feedback is also crucial for student growth. You can provide specific feedback on assignments, highlighting areas of strength and areas for improvement. For example, when reviewing a student's essay, you can praise their clear writing style while also offering suggestions for improving organization. This approach encourages students to take ownership of their learning and strive for continuous improvement.

Collaborating and involving students in decision-making processes can be achieved by incorporating group projects or class discussions where students share their ideas and opinions. For example, when planning a class project, you can ask students for input on the topic, format, and timeline. This collaborative approach fosters a sense of ownership and commitment among students, leading to enhanced engagement and motivation.

You will also need respectful conflict resolution. This involves addressing disagreements respectfully and constructively. For instance, if two students have a disagreement during a group activity, you can facilitate a discussion where they express their concerns assertively and work together to find a solution. This teaches students valuable problem-solving skills and promotes a culture of respect and understanding in the classroom, a place where it's safe to disagree.

Additionally, providing personalized support and recognition can be as simple as acknowledging your students' efforts and achievements. For example, you can praise a student for their participation in a class discussion or provide extra help to a student who is struggling with a concept. This personalized approach fosters a sense of value and motivation among students, ensuring that every student feels supported and empowered no matter where they're at in the process.

To further enhance positive relationships through assertiveness, consider incorporating activities that promote teamwork, communication skills, and problem-solving abilities. For example, you can organize group projects that require collaboration and effective communication. Such activities will encourage students to work together towards common goals. This creates a positive and inclusive classroom culture where diversity is celebrated, and every student's voice is heard and valued.

By implementing these strategies consistently in your teaching practice, you can create an environment where every student feels valued, supported, and empowered to succeed. Your assertiveness in building positive relationships will foster a sense of belonging, promote academic growth, and cultivate a community where everyone thrives. As you build these relationships, you'll also want to examine the benefits of such connections.

Benefits of Fostering Connection With Students

Building positive relationships with students goes beyond immediate classroom interactions; it lays the groundwork for lifelong benefits that extend far beyond academic achievement. One of the key aspects of fostering these connections is the development of emotional intelligence (EQ) in students. Research consistently shows that students who have positive relationships with their teachers tend to achieve higher academically, feel more motivated, and have better self-esteem. Why is that? For starters, when you make your students feel supported and valued, they're more likely to take academic risks, ask questions, and actively engage in classroom activities. This heightened engagement not only deepens their learning but also makes their school experience more positive and fulfilling.

Emotional intelligence encompasses the ability to recognize, understand, and manage emotions effectively, both in oneself and others. For teachers, EQ plays a pivotal role in shaping student-teacher relationships and overall learning outcomes. When teachers are emotionally attuned to their students, they're better equipped to create a positive and inclusive classroom environment. Understanding the impact of emotions on learning allows teachers to support students in managing their emotions, thus facilitating a conducive learning environment. Emotional intelligence is actually complementary to assertiveness, which we discussed earlier, as it enhances the ability to understand and manage emotions effectively. In turn, this supports assertive communication, fosters positive relationships, and creates a conducive learning environment.

Increasing your EQ involves self-awareness, self-regulation, empathy, and effective communication. Self-awareness means recognizing your emotions, strengths, weaknesses, and triggers, allowing you to manage your responses effectively. Self-regulation involves controlling your impulses, managing stress, and adapting to changing circumstances without letting emotions dictate your actions. Empathy is essential for understanding your students' perspectives, feelings, and needs, fostering a sense of connection and trust. Effective communication involves clear expression, active listening, and constructive feedback, promoting healthy interactions and relationship building.

Beyond EQ, social-emotional learning (SEL) is a benefit

as well. SEL focuses on nurturing students' emotional intelligence and interpersonal skills. It encompasses a range of skills and competencies that are crucial for personal and academic success. It involves teaching your students how to recognize and manage their emotions, develop empathy and social awareness, establish and maintain positive relationships, make responsible decisions, and handle interpersonal conflicts effectively. It's a big task that pays big dividends. This holistic approach not only enhances students' emotional well-being but also equips them with essential life skills that are integral to their personal and academic success.

SEL has the potential to help your students develop a greater understanding of their emotions, leading to improved emotional regulation and mental well-being. It can equip them with coping strategies to manage stress, anxiety, and other challenges. SEL fosters the development of essential social skills such as communication, cooperation, empathy, and conflict resolution. These skills are vital for building healthy relationships and navigating social interactions both in and out of school.

Unsurprisingly, research shows that students with strong social-emotional skills perform better academically. They are more engaged in learning, exhibit better behavior in the classroom, and demonstrate higher levels of motivation and persistence.

SEL provides students with practical life skills that are valuable beyond the classroom. This includes (but isn't limited to) problem-solving skills, decision-making skills, self-awareness, resilience, and responsible behavior.

By promoting a positive and supportive school climate, SEL contributes to a more inclusive and welcoming environment where students feel safe, respected, and valued. By integrating SEL into your curriculum and classroom practices, you create a nurturing and empowering learning environment. When your students' holistic development is supported, then they are prepared for success in school and beyond.

You are the key to this. That's because relationships with teachers have been shown to significantly contribute to students' mental health and well-being. When students feel supported, they experience lower levels of anxiety, depression, and other mental health issues. This positive impact on mental health extends beyond the classroom and influences students' overall happiness and life satisfaction.

Moreover, strong teacher-student relationships foster a sense of accountability and responsibility for students. When they know their teachers care about their success and well-being, they are more motivated to set goals, work hard, and persevere through challenges. This intrinsic motivation leads to greater self-discipline, resilience, and a growth mindset essential for long-term success.

As you can see, the benefits of fostering connection with students are multifaceted and profound. From academic achievement and emotional well-being to personal growth and life skills, positive relationships with teachers lay the foundation for a brighter future for students. As educators, investing in these connections not only enhances student outcomes but also brings joy, fulfillment, and purpose to your teaching journey. As you build these connections, you will develop a good rapport with your students.

Building Trust and Rapport with Students

Building trust and rapport with students is a cornerstone of effective teaching that lays the foundation for a positive and productive learning environment. When students trust and feel connected to their teachers, they are more engaged, motivated, and receptive to learning. Let's explore the importance of building trust and rapport with students, strategies to strengthen these connections, and the impact they have on student success.

Importance of Building Trust and Rapport

Trust and rapport are essential components of a successful teacher-student relationship. When students trust their teachers, they feel safe to express their thoughts, ask questions, and take academic risks. This trust creates a supportive environment where students are more likely to participate actively in class discussions, collaborate with peers, and seek help when needed. Additionally, when teachers have strong rapport with their students, they can better understand their individual needs, interests, and learning styles, leading to more personalized and effective instruction.

Building trust and rapport also fosters a positive classroom culture. Students are more likely to follow rules, engage in positive behaviors, and contribute to the learning community when they have a strong rapport with their teacher. Moreover, this contributes to a sense of belonging and emotional well-being among students, critical factors for academic success and overall student development.

Are you eager to get started, and you're wondering what this might look like in your classroom? Here are six key strategies you can use to build rapport with your students:

1. **Get to Know Your Students:** Take the time to learn about your students' backgrounds, interests, strengths, and challenges. Show genuine interest in their lives and experiences. Use this knowledge to tailor your teaching approach and provide personalized support.

2. **Be Approachable and Available:** Create a welcoming and supportive classroom environment where students feel comfortable approaching you with questions, concerns, or ideas. Be accessible during and after class. Then, encourage open communication through regular check-ins and feedback sessions.

3. **Establish Clear Expectations:** Set clear and consistent expectations for behavior, academic performance, and classroom procedures. Communicate these expectations early on and reinforce them regularly to create a structured and predictable learning environment.

4. **Show Empathy and Understanding:** Demonstrate understanding towards your students' feelings, experiences, and challenges. Be sensitive to their individual needs and circumstances. Then, provide support and encouragement when they face difficulties.

5. **Build Positive Relationships:** Foster positive relationships with your students based on mutual respect and trust. Use positive reinforcement, praise, and encouragement to recognize their efforts and achievements. Before you know it, you'll celebrate their successes together.

6. **Be Authentic and Genuine:** Be yourself and show authenticity in your interactions with students. Share your own experiences, passions, and interests. Consider how you can create opportunities for meaningful connections and shared experiences.

Impact on Student Success

Building trusted relationships with students has a profound impact on their academic success, well-being, and overall development. Students who feel connected to their teachers are more likely to attend classes regularly, actively participate in discussions, and exhibit positive behaviors. They are also more motivated to learn, take ownership of their education, and set higher goals for themselves. In other words, while your students may be hard to motivate, your good rapport with them will naturally motivate them.

Strong teacher-student relationships contribute to improved student outcomes, including higher grades, test scores, and graduation rates. Students who have positive relationships with their teachers are also more resilient in the face of challenges, more confident in their abilities, and more engaged in school activities and extracurriculars.

Moreover, the journey of building positive relationships in the classroom is a transformative experience that shapes not only students' academic success but also their overall well-being and personal growth.

As educators, our role goes beyond delivering lessons; it encompasses creating a nurturing environment where every student feels valued, supported, and empowered to thrive. The benefits of fostering connection with students are vast, ranging from improved academic performance and emotional well-being to the development of essential life skills like empathy, communication, and resilience.

The journey of building positive relationships involves getting to know each student's unique strengths, challenges, and aspirations, fostering a sense of belonging and inclusion, and creating opportunities for meaningful connections and shared experiences. It requires active listening, empathy, clear communication, and a genuine commitment to understanding and meeting students' needs.

The story of Jake serves as a poignant reminder of the transformative power of genuine care, connection, and emotional intelligence in education. By investing in positive relationships with our students, we not only enhance their educational experience but also contribute to a more compassionate, supportive, and thriving learning community.

As we continue on this journey, let us remember that every interaction, every conversation, and every connection matters. By prioritizing relationships before rigor, we lay the foundation for a brighter future where every student can reach their full potential and lead fulfilling lives.

Together, let us embrace the power of positive relationships in education and create a legacy of care, empathy, and empowerment that shapes the hearts and minds of generations to come.

3

Educere: Building Strengths, Passions, and a Growth Mindset

Having spent over three decades immersed in the field of education, one thing has become abundantly clear. The prevailing focus of our education system has shifted towards fixing weaknesses in students rather than nurturing and guiding them to reach their full potential. My question is why? Why have we transformed into a system that prioritizes addressing deficits over fostering the inherent strengths and talents of each learner?

When I taught life science, I encountered students who weren't necessarily strong academically or who didn't particularly enjoy science. Recognizing this, I made it a priority to make the class as engaging as possible. One strategy I employed was taking the students outdoors once every week or so for team-building activities. This not only got them out of the classroom but also allowed me to tap into their strengths in leadership, critical thinking, and teamwork.

I noticed a remarkable transformation among these students.

As they excelled in these activities and felt successful, they began to look forward to the class more, knowing that if they worked hard and did their best, they would have the opportunity to participate in these outdoor activities. It worked. This positive reinforcement not only boosted their enthusiasm for science but also improved their overall performance in the subject.

Contrarily, many students across the nation leave school each day feeling defeated and deflated because the focus is consistently on their weaknesses rather than their strengths. This widespread approach can contribute to students developing a negative perception of school and struggling to find motivation or enjoyment in the educational experience. By shifting our focus to highlight and cultivate students' strengths, we can create a more positive and empowering learning environment for all students.

This raises a profound question about the purpose of education. Is it solely about bringing students up to a predefined standard, or should it be a dynamic and personalized journey that empowers everyone to discover, refine, and excel in their unique capabilities?

The latter perspective aligns more closely with the principles of a growth mindset, emphasizing the limitless potential for development and achievement. By shifting the educational paradigm towards a growth mindset, educators can play a pivotal role in unlocking the untapped potential within each student. This involves moving away from a singular focus on weaknesses and adopting an approach that celebrates and develops the unique capabilities of individuals.

Recognizing and implementing strategies that prioritize the identification and development of students' distinctive qualities can establish an environment that goes beyond the mere transmission of knowledge. This practical approach not only facilitates academic growth but also fosters a genuine appreciation for the diversity of individual strengths, guiding students toward a path of comprehensive development and achievement.

The Educere philosophy, rooted in the Latin concept of "to

lead or bring out," challenges educators to shift their focus from a one-size-fits-all model to one that recognizes and amplifies individual aptitudes. It prompts a departure from the standard educational narrative that often fixates on weaknesses, steering toward an approach that spotlights and cultivates the diverse strengths, talents, and passions that students bring into the learning environment.

Understanding the Concept of Educere in the Classroom

Educere is exemplified by recognizing that every student harbors talents and abilities that can lead them to greatness. This perspective asserts that each student possesses a unique set of talents, strengths, and passions waiting to be uncovered. This is extra powerful because it aligns with and leads to a growth mindset.

The key is creating an environment that promotes self-discovery and a love for learning. For instance, implementing team-building activities encourages students to tap into their unique strengths. Nurturing a student's leadership, critical thinking, and teamwork, can foster a positive and inclusive classroom culture.

This approach places a profound emphasis on directing attention and shaping perceptions. By encouraging educators to focus on the unique qualities and strengths of each student, it creates a lens through which potential is recognized and celebrated. This intentional shift challenges traditional perceptions of education by recognizing that learning is not a one-size-fits-all endeavor. It urges educators to perceive each student as a dynamic individual with a distinctive learning journey, fostering an inclusive and empowering environment where diversity is embraced, and every student's unique qualities become a source of strength.

Albert Einstein's quote about everyone being a genius but in different ways serves as a profound reflection on the contrast between a growth mindset and a fixed mindset. The analogy of judging a fish by its ability to climb a tree illustrates how rigid evaluations based on limited criteria can lead individuals to believe in their own limitations. This perspective is reminiscent of the fixed mindset, where one's abilities are seen as static and constrained by predetermined standards.

On the other hand, the Educere approach aligns with the principles of a growth mindset. It emphasizes the importance of recognizing and nurturing diverse talents, rejecting the notion of uniform standards that may not accommodate everyone's unique strengths. This mindset encourages educators to understand each student's capabilities holistically, fostering an environment where individual potential can thrive.

In the context of education, a growth mindset involves actively challenging cognitive biases that may hinder personal development. By focusing on students' strengths and abilities, educators can guide students towards realizing their fullest potential. This approach not only counters biases that stem from a fixed mindset but also opens a world of possibilities where limitations are replaced by opportunities for growth and achievement.

Furthermore, the connection between the growth mindset and the law of attraction highlights the power of positive thinking in shaping experiences and outcomes. Embracing a growth mindset involves cultivating a positive outlook on learning, embracing challenges as opportunities for development, and persisting in the face of setbacks. This positive mindset resonates with the law of attraction's emphasis on the transformative effects of positive thinking, reinforcing the idea that our beliefs and attitudes play a crucial role in shaping our experiences.

The key lies not only in recognizing individuality but also in exploring who students are as learners.

The goal is to empower individuals to actively engage in their learning journey, acquiring knowledge, developing skills, and gaining confidence to navigate their paths. Through this approach, learners become self-directed, critical thinkers capable of making meaningful contributions to society—a philosophy that closely mirrors the growth mindset's emphasis on continuous learning and development.

In the realm of teaching and learning, educators need to recognize the dynamic nature of students' interests and strengths. We can remain open to evolving our teaching methods, adapting to the changing landscape of students' needs and aspirations. We can champion methods such as project-based learning, experiential education, and personalized instruction. This adaptability ensures that the learning experience remains vibrant and evolving, fostering a more meaningful and enduring educational experience.

This transformative approach prioritizes the holistic development of individuals, guiding them toward self-discovery and nurturing a lifelong love for learning. It transcends conventional education paradigms, focusing on illuminating individual potential and cultivating well-rounded, empowered individuals—echoing the essence of a growth mindset in fostering a positive and resilient attitude towards learning and personal development.

Implementing Educere in the Classroom

Incorporating Educere into lesson planning and curriculum design is the cornerstone of fostering a growth mindset within the classroom. This intentional approach aligns educational content with students' interests and strengths, creating a dynamic and engaging learning environment. It is also attainable. You can do this in your classroom too.

Through the infusion of hands-on activities, project-based learning, and real-world applications into lessons, you can inspire students to connect their learning to personal experiences and future aspirations while you also lay the foundation for cultivating a growth mindset.

For example, Project-Based Learning (PBL) engages students in collaborative, real-world projects that require them to investigate, analyze, and solve complex problems. It emphasizes inquiry, critical thinking, and the application of knowledge and skills in a practical context. You could design a PBL project where your students collaborate to address a real-world environmental issue in your community. They could conduct in-depth research, propose sustainable solutions, and present their findings to the class or community stakeholders. This holistic approach would foster a deep understanding of the subject matter and leave your students empowered.

Another great strategy you can employ is Inquiry-Based Learning. It empowers students to explore topics by posing open-ended questions, encouraging curiosity, critical thinking, and independent research. It promotes a student-driven approach to learning. For instance, you might implement Inquiry-Based Learning by encouraging your students to explore open-ended questions related to a historical event, stimulating independent thinking and research, allowing students to draw meaningful conclusions, and present their findings in a format of their choice, fostering a sense of ownership in their learning journey.

Cooperative Learning is another outstanding strategy, especially as it builds relationships between classmates. It involves students working together in small groups to achieve a shared objective. As you might expect, it emphasizes collaboration, communication, and the development of interpersonal skills. You could organize a Cooperative Learning activity where students work in small groups to create a multimedia presentation on a science topic, assigning specific roles within the group to promote collaboration, communication, and shared responsibility, to foster a positive team dynamic.

One effective tool for evaluating students is the Authentic Assessment. It allows you to evaluate your students' understanding through real-world applications. It goes beyond traditional testing methods and emphasizes the practical application of knowledge and skills in authentic contexts. Instead of a traditional written test, you could have your students create a podcast episode to analyze characters, themes, and plot developments in a novel, mirroring real-world communication skills and application.

If you're wanting more of an independent project, you might utilize Choice-Based Assignments. They provide students with autonomy by allowing them to select topics or formats that align with their interests and strengths, emphasizing personalized learning experiences and student agency. For instance, in a literature assignment, you could have students choose between writing a traditional essay, creating a visual representation, or recording a dramatic interpretation related to the same novel. This strategy accommodates diverse learning styles, allowing students to showcase their strengths.

Student-Led Discussions are another great way to empower your students. In this strategy, students get to take turns leading conversations, expressing their ideas and perspectives, encouraging active participation, critical thinking, and leadership skills. Designating one day each week for student-led discussions fosters a sense of ownership and leadership among students, promoting a deeper understanding of the topics through peer-led exploration.

For a more-autonomous strategy, you may choose Independent Research. This open-ended research allows students to research a topic of their choice. It fosters self-directed learning, critical thinking, and a deeper understanding of subject matter. For example, an independent research project could involve students selecting a historical figure, delving into their life and contributions, and presenting their findings through a multimedia presentation, encouraging self-directed exploration and critical analysis.

The implementation of Educere strategies in lesson planning and curriculum design not only makes learning more engaging and relevant but also actively nurtures a growth mindset among students. By emphasizing curiosity, collaboration, and the application of knowledge in real-world contexts, you can play a pivotal role in instilling the belief that intelligence and abilities are not fixed but can be developed through dedication and resilience. These strategies provide a multifaceted approach to education, helping you cater to diverse learning styles and fostering an empowering learning environment.

The Benefits of Educere in Student Learning

When students are given the opportunity to explore and develop their talents, strengths, and passions, remarkable things happen. They become more engaged, motivated, and invested in their own learning journey. By tapping into their innate abilities, students gain a deeper sense of purpose and fulfillment. They become more confident in their capability as an individual, which in turn leads to higher academic achievement.

Educere in the classroom also helps students develop a strong sense of self-awareness. As they explore their talents and passions, they gain a better understanding of who they are and what they can achieve. This self-awareness not only benefits their academic performance but also prepares them for future success in their personal and professional lives.

Enhanced student engagement is a cornerstone of this approach, igniting a passion for knowledge that transcends mere academic pursuits. Encouraging students to explore their talents and passions taps into their intrinsic motivation, curiosity, and genuine interest in acquiring knowledge. This active involvement leads to increased retention, deeper understanding, and a lifelong love for learning.

Recognizing and celebrating each student's unique identity and potential is central to this approach. Creating a personalized learning environment facilitates not only academic excellence but also essential life skills such as self-confidence, critical thinking, and resilience. Tailored feedback and opportunities for self-reflection contribute to a holistic understanding of oneself and capabilities, laying a strong foundation for success.

Empowering students to think critically, creatively, and analytically is another significant aspect. Inquiry-based learning, collaborative problem-solving, and real-world applications of knowledge develop cognitive skills and competencies essential for navigating complex challenges. Independent exploration, evaluating multiple perspectives, and generating innovative solutions foster adept problem solvers ready for the challenges of the 21st century.

The profound outcome of this approach is the journey of self-discovery it fosters in students. Encouraging them to explore interests, strengths, and aspirations enables a deeper understanding of values and goals. This heightened self-awareness becomes a guiding force in academic pursuits, personal growth, and decision-making, empowering informed choices and paths aligned with a student's passions.

Creating a nurturing and inclusive learning environment where every student feels valued, respected, and supported is vital. Celebrating diversity, encouraging collaboration, and fostering a sense of belonging cultivates positive social interactions, mutual support, and a strong sense of community. This inclusive atmosphere enhances learning outcomes and promotes empathy, understanding, and respect for diverse perspectives.

Equipping students with essential skills, competencies, and mindsets needed for success in a rapidly changing world is fundamental. From adaptability and resilience to communication and collaboration, developing a versatile skill set prepares students to navigate the complexities of the modern world with confidence and agility. Integrating future-focused learning experiences ensures readiness to thrive in diverse contexts and seize opportunities for growth and innovation.

Emphasizing the practical application of knowledge bridges

the gap between theory and practice. Connecting classroom concepts to real-world scenarios demonstrates the relevance and impact of education in solving real-life problems. Experiential learning opportunities, internships, and community engagement initiatives help students develop a deep appreciation for the practical utility of knowledge, making learning meaningful and relevant to real life.

Encouraging students to embrace challenges as opportunities for growth and learning fosters a growth mindset. Promoting risk-taking and providing support through setbacks empower resilience, perseverance, and adaptability. Navigating uncertainties and overcoming obstacles with confidence and determination nurtures continuous improvement and readiness for dynamic environments.

In essence, prioritizing students' needs and interests transforms the learning experience by fostering engagement, personalized development, critical thinking, self-awareness, inclusivity, future readiness, real-world application, and resilience. Embracing these principles empowers students to unlock their full potential, become lifelong learners, and contribute meaningfully to society as informed, empowered citizens.

Through the cultivation of individual strengths, passions, and skills, Educere prepares students to excel academically and navigate the complexities of the modern world with resilience and creativity.

How might this look in your classroom? In a science class, you could have students work on a long-term project to design and conduct experiments, which would foster resilience in the face of scientific challenges. In an art class, you could have students explore various mediums and techniques, nurturing their creative thinking and problem-solving skills. Similarly, you could engage them in project-based learning in history class, deepening their appreciation for inquiry and critical thinking. On the other hand, coding projects in technology class could enhance their adaptability to evolving landscapes. Lastly, participating in peer feedback sessions in language arts class could build your students' confidence and enthusiasm for continuous learning and growth.

These are just a few examples that showcase how you could use Educere to equip your students. You have the power to teach them these essential qualities to thrive in an ever-changing world, paving the way for a generation empowered to meet future challenges with confidence and enthusiasm.

Unlocking Potential Through Strengths and Passion

When schools focus on weaknesses, students feel defeated, resulting in limited success. By shifting the focus to helping students through their strengths and passions, you can pave the way for a dynamic and fulfilling educational journey that transcends traditional classroom boundaries. This intentional focus not only propels students towards success but also ignites a transformative journey of self-discovery and resilience. Let's dig deeper into the five interconnected steps that explain the profound impact of prioritizing strengths and passions in education.

Step 1: Unleashing Potential Through Strengths and Passions

Encouraging students to identify and nurture their strengths and passions lays the cornerstone for a transformative educational experience. As an educator, you serve as a mentor, guiding students to celebrate their unique abilities.

For example, a student who excels in visual arts may struggle in traditional subjects but can shine when projects integrate artistic expression. By providing such opportunities, you can tap into your students' strengths and passions, fostering a sense of accomplishment and engagement that transcends traditional academic barriers.

Step 2: Empowering Success Through Strengths

Because traditional education approaches focus on weaknesses, students quickly check out. However, when students experience success through their strengths, it becomes a powerful source of motivation and self-assurance. Imagine one of your students who struggles with traditional writing tasks but excels in storytelling through multimedia presentations. By leveraging this strength, your student can achieve success while gaining confidence and a positive attitude towards learning.

Step 3: Building Confidence Grounded in Success

Confidence is built through experiencing success. When students achieve milestones and overcome challenges using their strengths, they develop a genuine sense of confidence. Consider a student who's passionate about technology but struggles with public speaking. However, they could thrive if given the opportunity to present tech-related projects. By providing the opportunity and then celebrating these successes, you could help students build resilience and self-belief, laying a solid foundation for future endeavors.

Step 4: Embracing Challenges and Growth

Encouraging students to use their strengths when facing challenges transforms obstacles into opportunities for growth. You can emphasize the importance of resilience and proactive risk-taking, instilling a mindset where challenges are viewed as stepping stones to further development. Consider a student who loves sports but struggles with time management. By incorporating sports-themed organizational strategies, such as setting goals like game schedules, you can empower your student to overcome challenges while staying true to their passions.

Step 5: Cultivating Lifelong Learning and Continuous Improvement

The mindset cultivated through focusing on strengths and passions extends beyond formal education, fostering a lifelong commitment to learning and improvement. Students equipped with this approach become avid learners, navigating complexities with curiosity and resilience. As their guide on this journey, you can instill the belief that learning is a continuous process. This can maximize your students' potential for success in all aspects of life. For example, your student passionate about environmental issues could start a sustainability club in high school, leading to lifelong advocacy and learning in environmental sciences.

By embracing strengths and passions, you not only enhance academic achievement but also empower your students to navigate life's challenges. This approach, rooted in celebrating individual uniqueness, lays the foundation to help students maximize their potential and become their best self.

As you move forward, prioritizing your students' strengths and passions in education, there are three key strategies that will help. Firstly, conducting strengths assessments can provide invaluable insights into each student's unique talents and interests, paving the way for personalized lesson planning that aligns with their strengths and passions. This approach not only enhances engagement but also empowers students to take ownership of their learning journey. For example, there are assessments such as *StrengthsExplorer for Ages*

10-14 or *Emotional Intelligence Assessments for Kids* which can help them find their strengths.

Secondly, creating a supportive classroom environment that celebrates diversity and encourages risk-taking plays a pivotal role in fostering holistic development. By fostering a culture of respect, collaboration, and acceptance, you can nurture a sense of belonging and confidence among students, enabling them to thrive academically and emotionally.

Lastly, providing opportunities for students to showcase their strengths through projects, presentations, or collaborative activities can significantly boost their sense of accomplishment and intrinsic motivation. These opportunities not only allow students to demonstrate their talents but also encourage them to explore new interests and push their boundaries, leading to a deeper and more meaningful learning experience.

4

Unveiling the Pygmalion Effect in Education

In the intricate relationship between teacher expectations and student achievement, the Pygmalion Effect offers profound implications for the educational landscape. Drawing inspiration from George Bernard Shaw's timeless play, *Pygmalion*, we can begin to unravel the layers of this effect and understand how a teacher's beliefs in their students can sculpt the classroom narrative.

During college, I had the privilege of studying *Pygmalion* in a literature class taught by a retired nun. Her unique life experience, perspective, and teaching style added depth and a rich context to our exploration of the Pygmalion Effect, making it more than just a theoretical concept but a real-world phenomenon with tangible implications for education. Additionally, as a nun, she taught the importance of seeing the best in others, further enriching our understanding of human potential and the impact of positive expectations.

Shaw's *Pygmalion* weaves a narrative around Professor Henry Higgins and his ambitious experiment to transform Eliza

Doolittle, a humble flower girl, into a refined lady. The crux of the story lies not only in the professor's ability to shape Eliza's outward appearance but, more significantly, in how his expectations shape her own perception of herself. In this theatrical masterpiece, the Pygmalion Effect is palpable, illustrating the transformative power of believing in someone's untapped potential.

As Professor Higgins endeavors to refine Eliza, the audience witnesses the unfolding impact of his expectations on her self-image and capabilities. The shaping of Eliza's identity, not merely because of external changes but as a direct consequence of the professor's beliefs, serves as a poignant metaphor for the potential within each student waiting to be unlocked by a trustworthy guide.

Like Professor Higgins, educators play a pivotal role in shaping the destinies of their students through the lens of expectations. In education, the Pygmalion Effect encapsulates the idea that students often live up to their teacher's expectations, whether those expectations are explicit or subtly conveyed through non-verbal cues.

In fact, a teacher's perception of their students can become a self-fulfilling prophecy. Whether viewing a student as gifted and capable or struggling and challenged, the expectations communicated by educators can significantly influence students' beliefs about their own capabilities. It's time to illuminate the psychological mechanisms at play, shedding light on how teacher expectations can act as a powerful catalyst for student success or, conversely, a potential hindrance.

By cultivating a belief in the untapped potential within each student, educators can foster an environment where expectations serve as stepping stones, guiding students towards achievements they may not have deemed possible. Through this exploration, we aim to empower educators to become conscious architects of positive expectations, molding narratives of success and unlocking the latent capabilities within each student.

Pygmalion in the Classroom

The Pygmalion Effect holds profound significance in the realm of education, especially within the classroom setting. One classic example often cited to reflect the Pygmalion Effect in education is the "Rosenthal-Jacobson Study," also known as the Pygmalion in the Classroom study, conducted in the 1960s by psychologists Robert Rosenthal and Lenore Jacobson.

This groundbreaking study brought to light the profound influence of teacher expectations on students' intellectual growth. This study delves into the Pygmalion Effect, wherein teachers' expectations significantly impact the academic performance of their students.

Study Overview

The study, conducted in a California elementary school, aimed to explore the correlation between teachers' expectations and students' intellectual development. Rosenthal and Jacobson hypothesized that when teachers maintained high expectations for their students, those expectations would become self-fulfilling prophecies, influencing the students' actual achievements. They sought to uncover the extent to which teachers' expectations could impact students' intellectual growth, shedding light on the potential influence of those expectations on academic outcomes. By examining that dynamic, researchers aimed to provide valuable insights into the ways in which teacher-student interactions and expectations could shape students' educational trajectories.

Methodology

To test their hypothesis, the researchers administered an IQ test to all students at the beginning of the academic year. Unbeknownst to the teachers, the researchers randomly labeled a group of students as "academic spurters" based on the test results. Importantly, some of the students labeled as "academic spurters" had scored low on the IQ test, while others had scored high. However, the label was presented to the teachers indiscriminately, regardless of the actual test scores.

The study aimed to investigate the effects of teachers' expectations on students' progress while making the teachers aware of the specific students labeled as "academic spurters." Their approach allowed the researchers to observe how the teachers' expectations influenced the academic development of the identified students. It also provided valuable insights into the potential impact of those expectations on students' intellectual growth over the academic year. The study revealed that teachers exhibited higher expectations and provided more support and encouragement to the students they believed to be "academic spurters," regardless of their actual IQ test scores. This finding highlighted the significant impact of teachers' expectations on student outcomes, irrespective of the students' initial intellectual abilities.

Findings

The study yielded compelling results. At the end of the school year, the researchers found that the students labeled as "academic spurters" exhibited significantly greater intellectual development compared to their peers, despite no initial differences in their actual intellectual abilities. This significant disparity in intellectual growth highlighted the tangible impact of the teachers' positive expectations on the students' academic performance, providing empirical evidence of the Pygmalion Effect in action. These findings underscored the importance of cultivating a supportive and encouraging educational environment where positive expectations foster students' intellectual development and overall success.

Implications for Education

Rosenthal and Jacobson's study has profound implications for education, emphasizing the pivotal role teachers play in shaping students' perceptions of their own capabilities. The study suggests that when teachers maintain high expectations for their students, it fosters a conducive environment for learning and academic achievement. Conversely, **it also implies that low expectations can potentially impede students' intellectual development**, highlighting the need for educators to be mindful of their beliefs and attitudes toward students. The study's implications emphasize the critical role of educators in creating an environment that nurtures high expectations, recognizing the potential for these expectations to positively influence students' academic progress and accomplishments. By acknowledging the influence of teacher expectations, educators can strive to create an atmosphere that promotes positive student outcomes and fosters an environment conducive to intellectual growth and development.

Conclusion

Rosenthal and Jacobson's study remains a landmark exploration of the Pygmalion Effect and its implications for education and has been duplicated in many other settings, including with adults. It underscores the significant impact of teachers' expectations on students' intellectual development. Furthermore, it serves as a poignant reminder of the influential role teachers play in shaping not only the academic but also the psychological and emotional trajectories of their students.

The Pygmalion Effect, as exemplified in studies such as Rosenthal and Jacobson's, also accentuates that changes in students' performance **are not inherently linked to factors like homelife, ethnicity or socioeconomic status. Rather, the pivotal element is how teachers perceive and expect their students to excel academically.**

In the study, teachers, influenced by false information indicating certain students were destined to be "academic bloomers," adjusted their teaching methods and interactions accordingly. This shift in teaching approach, driven by heightened expectations, resulted in tangible improvements in the academic performance of the students.

In essence, the Pygmalion Effect underscores the profound influence of teacher expectations on teaching strategies and, consequently, on student outcomes. It emphasizes the significant role that the beliefs and expectations of authority figures, such as teachers, can play in shaping the performance and potential of individuals, irrespective of their background characteristics.

Finally, the Pygmalion Effect serves as a cautionary reminder of the potential pitfalls associated with low expectations. When educators harbor negative beliefs about a student's capabilities, it can become a self-fulfilling prophecy, limiting the student's potential and impeding their intellectual growth. Recognizing and mitigating the impact of these unconscious biases is essential for cultivating an inclusive and equitable learning environment.

Teacher Expectations on Student Performance and Factors Influencing Expectations

The role of the teacher-student relationship is crucial in shaping academic trajectories and unlocking each student's potential. At the heart of this dynamic is the Pygmalion Effect—a concept highlighting the substantial role of teacher expectations. Imagine a common scenario at the beginning of a school year where some teachers seek to identify potential troublemakers among their students. Labeling them as such might inadvertently set the stage for a self-fulfilling prophecy, shaping how they perceive themselves and ultimately perform academically. I personally never cared how the student behaved the year before, I made sure they all started in my class with a clean slate and fresh start. In fact, I would tell each class that I heard nothing but great things about them from previous teachers and that I was thrilled to be teaching them.

During a keynote speech at the Oklahoma Association of Elementary School Principals conference, a principal shared a powerful anecdote highlighting the impact of positive expectations on a student's behavior. The story began with a young boy named Brad entering the classroom during open house and introducing himself as "bad," with his mother nodding in agreement. However, the teacher responded by telling Brad that only good students were in her class, instilling a sense of positivity and belief in his potential. This positive interaction set the tone for the entire year, leading to minimal problems with Brad and showcasing the transformative effect of starting with positive expectations in the classroom.

Positive teacher expectations act as more than mere affirmations; they are a dynamic force propelling students toward excellence. For example, when you consistently communicate high expectations for a student's academic performance and reinforce your belief in their capabilities, it can instill a sense of confidence and motivation in the student. By instilling belief in students' inherent abilities and communicating these convictions effectively, you—as their teacher— lay the foundation for a classroom culture where confidence and motivation flourish. This emphasis on positive expectations not only fosters a conducive learning environment but also contributes to students' self-belief and academic motivation.

At the heart of the Pygmalion Effect lies the notion of a self-fulfilling prophecy. This phenomenon occurs when teachers set high expectations for excellence and consistently convey their belief in students' potential. As a result, students internalize these expectations, creating a powerful feedback loop where belief becomes the driving force behind student performance. This dynamic demonstrates how your expectations can significantly influence students' self-perception and academic performance, showcasing the transformative nature of self-fulfilling prophecies in the classroom and its profound impact on students' academic development.

Research shows the correlation between high teacher expectations and equally high academic performance. For example, when students are buoyed by the belief that success is not only possible but expected, they tend to engage more deeply in the learning process, resulting in elevated levels of achievement. This evidence supports the pivotal role of positive expectations in motivating students to strive to reach their full potential. Of course, this highlights the significant influence of teacher expectations on student achievement.

We need educators who actively nurture a culture of high expectations. Institutional factors play a vital role in optimizing student outcomes by aligning frameworks with a commitment to fostering excellence. For example, when educational institutions prioritize initiatives aimed at setting high expectations for all students, it creates an environment where teachers are empowered to set and uphold positive expectations. This contributes to a culture of academic excellence.

As you consider the factors shaping your expectations—past performance, teacher-student relationships, and institutional influences—it becomes evident that you hold the key to making a difference. By actively challenging preconceived notions and fostering positive beliefs in every student, you unlock their boundless potential. The journey prompts you to recognize your role in shaping futures, highlighting the simplicity of making a difference by believing in students and treating them as the great individuals they can become. The transformative impact lies not just in academic lessons but in the daily interactions that contribute to a culture of excellence, where every student is seen through a lens of potential, paving the way for success.

Strategies for Applying the Pygmalion Effect

Expectations play a crucial role in education, where teachers wield a profound influence over their students' academic performance. In essence, the Pygmalion Effect emphasizes how teachers' beliefs, attitudes, and expectations towards their students can significantly shape their educational outcomes.

To effectively leverage expectations in education, it is essential for teachers to establish strong relationships with their students. Building strong, trusting connections fosters a conducive environment for learning and growth. For instance, a teacher who invests time in understanding each student personally, demonstrates empathy towards their challenges, cultivates a supportive classroom atmosphere, and lays the groundwork for positive relationships. Active listening, encouragement, and approachability are key elements in creating a safe space where students feel valued and motivated to engage in their educational journey.

Moreover, fostering a growth mindset among students is instrumental in applying the Pygmalion Effect. A growth mindset revolves around the belief that intelligence and abilities can be developed through effort, perseverance, and learning from failures. Teachers can promote a growth mindset by acknowledging and praising students' efforts, strategies, and resilience in tackling academic challenges. By celebrating progress and emphasizing the importance of learning from mistakes, educators empower students to embrace challenges and view setbacks as opportunities for growth.

Setting high yet attainable goals is another pivotal strategy for leveraging expectations effectively. Ambitious goals provide students with direction, purpose, and motivation to excel academically. Encouraging students to strive for academic milestones beyond their current level of proficiency can ignite their passion for learning and push them to reach new heights. For instance, a teacher might challenge a proficient student in mathematics to explore advanced concepts or participate in mathematical competitions to broaden their skills.

Addressing implicit biases and stereotypes is imperative to create an inclusive and equitable learning environment. Implicit biases, often stemming from unconscious attitudes or beliefs, can influence teachers' expectations and perceptions of students, leading to disparities in educational outcomes. It is essential to actively challenge assumptions and stereotypes based on factors such as race, gender, socioeconomic background, or academic history. Providing equitable opportunities, acknowledging diverse perspectives, and celebrating students' individual strengths are essential steps in creating a place where every student feels valued and supported.

Furthermore, utilizing positive affirmations and encouragement can significantly impact students' self-confidence and self-esteem. Regularly incorporating affirmations such as "You are capable of overcoming challenges" or "Your hard work and dedication will lead to success" can help form a positive self-image and motivate students to persevere. Moreover, offering personalized encouragement based on students' strengths, achievements, and areas for growth can further boost their confidence and motivation to excel.

Promoting collaboration and support among students is another effective strategy in leveraging expectations. Collaborative learning experiences such as group projects, discussions, and peer mentoring programs encourage teamwork and a shared responsibility for learning outcomes. By facilitating opportunities for students to work together and learn from one another, educators can create a collaborative learning environment that enhances engagement and problem-solving skills.

Continual reflection on teaching practices is an integral component of enhancing educators' effectiveness. By regularly seeking feedback and participating in professional development opportunities, teachers can continuously refine their instructional strategies and create impactful learning experiences for their students.

Leveraging expectations in education requires a comprehensive approach that includes building positive relationships, fostering a growth mindset, setting ambitious yet attainable goals, and addressing biases and stereotypes. It also means utilizing positive affirmations, promoting collaboration and support, engaging in continual reflection and professional development, and creating a dynamic learning environment. This multifaceted strategy empowers educators to create powerful learning environments where every student can thrive.

Examples of the Pygmalion Effect in the Classroom

In your classroom, you can be the type of teacher who believes in your students' exceptional potential. Your consistent communication of **high expectations** can lead to student empowerment and motivation, resulting in improved performance. You can provide challenging assignments and offer additional support when needed, fostering a sense of capability and determination. This is because your belief in your students' abilities can inspire them to reach new academic heights.

Similarly, labeling one of your students as "gifted" influences your interactions, leading to exemplary work and high achievement as the student internalizes and fulfills your expectations. You can provide more opportunities for advanced learning, offer praise and encouragement, and expect outstanding outcomes. This positive labeling creates a **self-fulfilling prophecy** where your student strives to meet the high standards set, showcasing the powerful impact of positive expectations on student performance.

On the flip side, **behavioral expectations** can also shape student behavior in unexpected ways. If you expect a particular student to exhibit disruptive behavior, you may unconsciously treat the student differently, leading to a reinforcement of the initial assumption. This differential treatment can perpetuate a negative cycle where your student fulfills your expectations by displaying disruptive behavior, highlighting how beliefs about students' behavior can influence actual outcomes.

Feedback and reinforcement play a crucial role in the Pygmalion Effect. Providing consistent positive feedback to a student perceived as capable and talented reinforces the student's self-belief and encourages them to continue excelling. Conversely, if you provide limited or predominantly negative feedback, it can impact the student's confidence, motivation, and performance, aligning with your initial expectations. This example underscores the importance of positive reinforcement in fostering a conducive learning environment.

Introducing a **growth mindset** to students emphasizes the idea that intelligence and abilities can be developed through effort and perseverance. If you consistently praise your students' efforts, it fosters a belief in continuous improvement. This approach can encourage your students to embrace challenges and persist in their learning journey. That's when your students will develop a positive self-image and perform better academically, reflecting on your expectation of their growth and development.

Lastly, empowering student leadership through **high expectations** and meaningful roles cultivates responsibility, collaboration, and achievement. If you assign leadership roles and responsibilities within the classroom, it communicates trust and the opportunity to make a positive impact. Students who take on these roles feel valued, capable, and motivated to fulfill their responsibilities effectively. As you can imagine, this contributes to improved teamwork, engagement, and academic performance.

These examples illustrate the profound influence of teacher expectations and affirmations on student growth and success, highlighting the potential for unlocking greatness within every learner. By understanding and leveraging the Pygmalion Effect positively, you can create a supportive and empowering learning environment that fosters your students' potential. The impact of **high expectations**, a **growth mindset**, and **student leadership** underscores the transformative power of your belief and affirmation.

Ultimately, the Pygmalion Effect serves as a powerful lens through which we can understand the intricate dynamics of teacher expectations and their profound impact on student outcomes. As educators, our beliefs, attitudes, and expectations play a pivotal role in shaping the narratives of success and potential within our classrooms.

Imagine if every student was treated as if they were high achieving and taught accordingly. Picture the impact it would have not only on their academic performance but also on their self-esteem, confidence, and lifelong aspirations. When students are lifted by the belief that success is not only possible but expected, they tend to engage more deeply in the learning process, resulting in elevated levels of achievement.

The ripple effects of positive expectations extend far beyond academic achievements. They contribute to students' confidence, self-esteem, and belief in their abilities. This inclusive environment fosters a sense of belonging and encourages students to express themselves authentically, leading to greater engagement and participation in their educational journey. When students feel valued and supported, they are more likely to take risks, explore new ideas, and actively participate in classroom activities, leading to deeper learning and personal growth.

Best of all is the fact that you have the power to cultivate this change, because it's your affirmation and expectation that they need.

5

Empowering Classrooms: Reframing Behaviors for Positive Learning Environments

Thomas Edison's journey as a student was marked by struggle and frustration. Considered a poor student by conventional standards, Edison faced challenges in traditional educational settings. His difficulties were highlighted when a schoolmaster labeled him as "addled," a term that ignited his mother's fierce determination.

Edison's mother, recognizing his potential and refusing to accept the negative label, withdrew him from school and took on the responsibility of his education at home. Years later, reflecting on the pivotal role his mother played in his life, Edison remarked, "My mother was the making of me. She was so true, so sure of me, and I felt I had someone to live for, someone I must not disappoint" (Martin, 1990, p. 8). This anecdote underscores the transformative power of positive expectations and unwavering support in shaping a student's trajectory.

Furthermore, Edison's experience underscores the importance of embracing diverse learning styles and reframing behaviors in education. Just as Edison's unconventional methods clashed with the rigid structures of his time, many students today may require alternative approaches to learning. Recognizing that traditional educational models may not accommodate every student's needs is crucial in fostering an inclusive environment that promotes growth and understanding. By adopting flexible teaching strategies and reframing behaviors as strengths rather than limitations, educators can create a space where every student feels valued and empowered to reach their full potential.

Reframing behaviors requires a shift in mindset. Instead of labeling disruptive students as difficult or problematic, educators should strive to understand the underlying motivations behind their actions. Perhaps they are seeking intellectual stimulation or challenging the status quo. By acknowledging and validating their perspectives, we can create a safe space for exploration and encourage them to channel their disruptive tendencies into productive endeavors.

Moreover, reframing behaviors involves empowering students to take ownership of their learning. Instead of being passive recipients of information, they should be active participants in their education. This can be achieved through project-based learning, where students are encouraged to ask questions, think critically, and solve real-world problems. By giving students the freedom to pursue their interests and explore their passions, we can tap into their innate curiosity and drive for knowledge.

In addition, reframing behaviors requires fostering a sense of empathy and understanding among students and educators alike. By promoting a culture of respect and inclusivity, we can create an environment where differences are celebrated and individual strengths are valued. We can achieve this through open dialogue, peer mentoring programs, and collaborative projects that encourage teamwork and cooperation.

Ultimately, reframing behaviors is about creating a paradigm shift in education. It is about recognizing that disruptive behaviors can be a sign of untapped potential and a call for change. By embracing diverse learning styles, empowering students, and fostering empathy, we can create a positive learning environment where every student's unique brilliance is recognized and nurtured.

As we embark on this journey of reframing behaviors, we need to remember the lessons of Thomas Edison. Let us embrace disruptions as opportunities for innovation, challenges as stepping stones for growth, and differences as the fuel for progress. In doing so, we can pave the way for a future where education is not a one-size-fits-all model but a dynamic and inclusive space that celebrates the diversity of learners and cultivates their full potential.

Shifting Perspective: Embracing Diverse Traits

The call to embrace diverse traits and behaviors is not only a philosophical standpoint but a necessity for creating dynamic and inclusive learning environments. This imperative becomes even more pronounced when we consider personality styles associated with low agreeableness—a dimension in the Five Factor Model of Personality characterized by tendencies such as competitiveness, questioning authority, stubbornness, and independence.

Questioning authority, often linked to low agreeableness, may be perceived as disruptive in a traditional classroom. However, reframing this trait as a positive aspect unveils its potential to foster critical thinking. Instead of suppressing the inclination to question, educators can create spaces where students can express their curiosity and challenge established ideas, transforming questioning authority into a tool for intellectual growth.

Stubbornness, another trait associated with low agreeableness, can be reframed as determination and resilience. Consider a student who has faced adversity and developed a stubborn determination to overcome obstacles. Instead of viewing this trait as an obstacle itself, educators can guide the student toward constructive endeavors. By acknowledging and channeling their persistence, educators help students develop resilience, essential for overcoming challenges and achieving long-term goals.

Independence, often associated with low agreeableness, is a trait that might be viewed through a negative lens in traditional educational settings. Independent students might be perceived as rebellious or non-compliant, challenging established norms. However, reframing independence as self-motivation and self-reliance unveils its positive potential. Independent learners can take initiative, explore their interests, and develop critical problem-solving skills. Educators, by recognizing and nurturing independence, empower students to become self-directed learners who actively seek knowledge and take ownership of their educational journey.

Understanding trauma is also vital in the process of reframing. One poignant example is a student who has experienced trauma, often expressing withdrawal or resistance to authority. Instead of viewing this behavior solely as disruptive, educators can recognize it as a potential indicator of trauma-related challenges.

Incorporating trauma-informed practices, educators can acknowledge their students' past experiences and create a safe space where they feel understood and supported. By approaching the situation with empathy and understanding, educators not only shift their perspective but also contribute to the healing process, fostering an environment where students can excel.

The importance of reframing these traits, especially in the context of trauma, lies not only in recognizing their positive aspects but also in encouraging educators to shift their mindset. Instead of seeing non-conforming behaviors as disruptions to be quelled, they should be viewed as indicators of untapped potential and unique perspectives arising from past experiences. Just as Thomas Edison's disruptive methods were initially met with skepticism, embracing diverse traits requires a paradigm shift in how we perceive and respond.

Educators play a pivotal role in this shift by creating an environment where differences are not only tolerated but celebrated. Open dialogue, peer mentoring programs, and collaborative projects become tools for fostering empathy and understanding, especially for students who have experienced trauma. By promoting a culture of respect and inclusivity, educators pave the way for an educational landscape that values individual strengths and recognizes that each student brings a unique brilliance to the collective tapestry of learning.

In conclusion, shifting perspective to embrace diverse traits is not just a philosophical stance; it is a practical approach to nurturing a positive learning environment. By reframing non-conforming behaviors and low agreeableness traits as positive factors, educators can unlock the full potential of each student, considering the impact of trauma on their experiences. This paradigm shift is not about dismissing disruptions but understanding them as calls for change and opportunities for growth. This ultimately paves the way for a future where education becomes a dynamic and inclusive space that celebrates the diversity of learners and cultivates their full potential.

The Power of Reframing in Classroom Management

In managing classrooms, it's important for teachers to see beyond just what students do on the surface. Instead of quickly labeling behaviors as good or bad, it's helpful to understand why students act the way they do. Sometimes, what seems like a problem behavior can actually be useful when we figure out what's behind it and how to deal with it. This approach not only makes classrooms more welcoming and caring but also helps teachers find better ways to support each student's learning and development.

We are often conditioned to see arguing as a negative trait, but it can be a valuable skill. For example, being effective at arguing is a desired skill for a lawyer, showcasing the real-world value of strong argumentative skills in professions where persuasion is crucial. If you were ever to need legal representation, you would undoubtedly hope that your lawyer is highly skilled and effective in arguing your case.

One of the key tenets of reframing in classroom management is the exploration beyond surface behaviors and labels. Often, students are hastily categorized based on observable actions, leading to a narrow understanding of their capabilities and potential. By investigating the motivations behind their behaviors, educators can unearth a wealth of information that provides valuable insights into each student's unique needs and challenges.

Consider the example of a student who exhibits frequent restlessness and fidgeting in class. In a traditional approach, this behavior might be labeled as disruptive, prompting corrective measures. However, through the lens of reframing, educators may uncover that the restlessness stems from a need for kinesthetic learning. By recognizing this underlying motivation, educators can introduce alternative learning methods that cater to the student's preferred style, transforming what was once perceived as disruptive into a pathway for enhanced engagement and understanding.

Moreover, reframing encourages educators to see beyond the immediate actions and labels associated with students. For instance, a student labeled as "defiant" may, in reality, be expressing a desire for autonomy and self-expression. By understanding the underlying motivation for defiance, educators can collaborate with the student to establish boundaries while providing opportunities for decision-making. This cultivates a much needed sense of empowerment and cooperation.

Reframing can also be a powerful tool for addressing interpersonal conflicts. Instead of perpetuating a cycle of punitive measures for students engaged in conflicts, educators can probe into the motivations behind the disputes. Perhaps a disagreement arises from a difference in communication styles or a need for validation. Through reframing, educators can facilitate open dialogue, teach conflict resolution skills, and transform conflicts into opportunities for growth and understanding.

Ultimately, the power of reframing in classroom management lies in its ability to humanize the educational experience. It encourages educators to perceive each student as an individual with a unique set of motivations, strengths, and challenges. By reframing behaviors, educators shift from a reactive stance to a proactive one. It makes it possible to implement interventions that address the root causes of behaviors rather than merely treating their manifestations.

In conclusion, reframing in classroom management is a paradigm shift that goes beyond surface behaviors and labels, inviting educators to explore the complex motivations that drive student actions. By understanding the underlying factors, educators can tailor interventions that not only address behavioral challenges but also cultivate positive outcomes and foster a supportive learning environment. Embracing the power of reframing opens the door to a more empathetic and effective approach to classroom management, where every student's potential is recognized and nurtured.

Navigating Challenging Behaviors: A Comprehensive Approach

Navigating challenging behaviors requires a multifaceted approach that goes beyond conventional disciplinary measures. As an educator, adopting a mindset of reframing can transform disruptive behaviors into opportunities for growth, autonomy, and meaningful engagement. This comprehensive strategy encompasses various dimensions of challenging behaviors, each requiring a tailored approach.

To effectively navigate disruptive behavior associated with low agreeableness traits, you must undergo a paradigm shift. Rather than viewing assertiveness and critical thinking as disruptions, recognize them as positive attributes. Embrace a growth mindset to guide students in channeling these traits constructively. This approach fosters an inclusive environment that values diverse personalities and perspectives.

By reframing the narrative, you can empower students to develop leadership skills, challenge conventional wisdom, and advocate for themselves and others. For instance, if you guide a student who displays assertiveness to lead a class discussion on a topic they are passionate about, it turns what was once perceived as disruptive into a constructive opportunity for leadership.

Practical strategies for redirecting disruptive energy involve creating meaningful classroom involvement. Collaborative projects, hands-on activities, and alternative methods of participation can capture the attention of students with low agreeableness traits. For example, if you task a student with assertiveness to lead a group project, it channels their energy into a collaborative effort that benefits the entire class.

Defiance, often perceived negatively, can be reframed as a sign of students' desire for autonomy. Acknowledge this autonomy-seeking behavior and redirect it towards responsible decision-making. Share scenarios where defiance leads to positive outcomes through responsible decision-making to shift the narrative from disobedience to self-regulation.

Strategies for guiding students toward responsible decision-making involve providing opportunities for autonomy. For instance, you can give a student labeled as defiant the responsibility of choosing a project topic within certain parameters. This not only addresses defiance but also nurtures a sense of responsibility and self-regulation in students.

Inattention can be reframed as a quest for relevance and meaningful learning experiences. If you recognize the underlying desire for connection and engagement, you can present lessons in a way that connects to your students' interests. This can increase engagement and refocus attention.

Methods for connecting lessons to students' interests involve incorporating real-world applications, multimedia, or interactive elements. For instance, you can incorporate multimedia presentations or a project that allows students to explore historical topics aligning with their personal interests. This approach not only addresses inattention but also cultivates curiosity and enthusiasm for learning.

As mentioned earlier, there can be positive aspects of argumentative behavior. Emphasize its role as a form of advocacy and critical thinking to reframe it from mere opposition to constructive expression. For example, you can showcase the real-world value of strong argumentative skills in professions where persuasion is crucial.

Creating constructive debates involves promoting critical thinking and maintaining a dynamic learning environment. Classroom debates that encourage respectful expression of differing viewpoints can be powerful tools. For instance, a structured debate on a relevant social issue can engage argumentative students in constructive discussions. Instances where fostering constructive argumentation led to increased participation and enthusiasm showcase the transformative potential of reframing.

Navigating challenging behaviors through the lens of reframing is a holistic approach that recognizes the positive potential within each student. By embracing diverse traits, fostering autonomy, and making lessons relevant, you can create a positive learning environment that not only addresses challenging behaviors but also cultivates a sense of empowerment and a new enthusiasm for learning.

Practical Strategies for Reframing Behaviors

Creating a positive classroom environment is essential for the growth and development of your students. As an educator, you have the power to shape the atmosphere within your classroom and influence the behaviors of your students. One effective approach to promoting positivity is by reframing behaviors. By shifting perspectives and transforming language, you can uncover the potential in each student. It can also foster a sense of empathy, understanding, and growth. It's time to explore the various techniques and strategies you can use to promote a positive classroom through the power of reframing behaviors.

Negative thought patterns can hinder your students' progress and significantly impact their overall well-being. For example, a student might consistently express, "I'm not good at math," reflecting a negative thought pattern. This belief can lead to self-doubt and reluctance to engage in math-related activities. As an educator, you can encourage self-reflection and introspection by guiding the student to question their assumptions. By challenging their perspective and highlighting their strengths in other subjects or problem-solving skills, you can help them reframe their negative thought pattern into a more positive one. This process empowers students to approach challenges with confidence and a growth mindset, ultimately contributing to a more positive classroom environment.

Assumptions are another aspect that can often lead to misunderstandings and conflicts in the classroom. For instance, if a student is consistently late to class, instead of assuming laziness or lack of respect, consider alternative explanations. Engage in a conversation with the student to understand if there are external factors like transportation issues or family responsibilities causing the tardiness. By encouraging students to seek alternative viewpoints and consider different perspectives, you can help them develop a more empathetic mindset. This not only cultivates a positive classroom but also promotes problem-solving skills among your students.

Incorporating mindfulness practices such as deep breathing exercises or mindfulness activities can help your students develop self-awareness, emotional regulation, and focus. For example, you could start each class with a brief mindfulness session where students practice deep breathing and centering techniques. This will help create a calm, centered classroom environment conducive to learning. Encourage students to use mindfulness techniques during challenging tasks or stressful situations as this will promote resilience and a positive mindset.

Teaching students effective conflict resolution skills, such as active listening, perspective-taking, and collaborative problem-solving, will empower them to resolve conflicts peacefully and respectfully. For instance, you could facilitate role-playing scenarios where students practice resolving conflicts using these skills. This not only enhances their communication and interpersonal skills but also nurtures empathy and cooperation. By promoting positive conflict resolution strategies, you can contribute to a harmonious and supportive classroom climate where students feel safe expressing their thoughts and resolving differences constructively.

Empathy plays a crucial role in promoting positive classrooms and building understanding and connection among students. For example, during a conflict in your class, you could facilitate a discussion where each student shares their perspective. Encourage active listening and prompt students to consider how the other person might be feeling. By promoting empathy through activities like role-playing or empathy-related discussions, your students will learn to see situations from different viewpoints and develop compassion towards others. This not only improves social interactions but also contributes to a supportive classroom environment where students feel valued and understood.

Perspective shifting is a powerful tool for reframing behaviors and promoting a growth-oriented mindset among students. As a teacher, you can help students see the bigger picture by encouraging them to consider different viewpoints and contexts. For instance, if a student struggles with a challenging assignment, prompt them to view it as an opportunity for growth and learning rather than an overwhelming task. By encouraging students to step outside their own experiences and understand the broader implications of their actions, you help them develop a more positive mindset. This approach not only enhances academic resilience but also promotes critical thinking and problem-solving skills essential for success.

The language we use in the classroom has a significant impact on the overall environment and student behavior. Transforming negative language into positive alternatives can promote a more hopeful atmosphere and create a sense of encouragement and support. For example, instead of labeling a student as "disruptive," consider describing their behavior as "enthusiastic" or "energetic." Encourage students to use words that uplift and inspire rather than criticize and discourage. By modeling positive language and providing feedback to students when they use negative language, you can create an encouraging classroom environment where students feel motivated and valued.

Adopting a strengths-based approach can further enhance positive behaviors and contribute to a motivated classroom environment. Instead of focusing solely on students' weaknesses and failures, emphasize their strengths and potential for growth. For example, if a student struggles with writing but excels in creativity, encourage them to channel their strengths into creative writing assignments. Provide opportunities for students to showcase their skills and talents, and celebrate their achievements, no matter how small. By focusing on your students' abilities and growth, you will create a positive classroom environment where students feel empowered to take on challenges.

Setting goals and fostering a goal-oriented mindset are essential aspects of promoting a positive classroom atmosphere. You can help your students identify their goals and create action plans to achieve them. For example, if a student aims to improve their grades, break down the goal into smaller, manageable steps like setting study schedules or seeking extra help. Celebrate their progress along the way and provide constructive feedback to keep them motivated. By encouraging goal-oriented thinking, you help your students develop a sense of purpose and determination, contributing to an achievement-focused environment where students are motivated to succeed and reach their full potential.

Creating a positive classroom environment is not just about teaching subjects; it's about shaping mindsets and fostering growth. As an educator, you hold the key to unlocking the potential within each student. By reframing behaviors, challenging assumptions, and promoting empathy, you can create a space where students feel valued, understood, and empowered. Through mindfulness practices, conflict resolution skills, and a strengths-based approach, you can help them cultivate resilience, creativity, and a positive outlook on learning.

Taking It Personally and Redirecting Constructively

Navigating student misbehavior is more than a professional challenge; it's a deeply personal journey. You invest not only your time and energy but also your emotions into nurturing your students' growth. When faced with misbehavior, it's natural to feel a personal connection to the situation.

Recognizing the personal impact of student misbehavior is crucial. It affects not just the learning process but also your emotional well-being. Disruptions in class can evoke feelings of disappointment and frustration. However, it's vital not to internalize these challenges. Internalization can lead to self-doubt and burnout, detracting from your ability to effectively support your students.

Effective strategies for addressing misbehavior involve a holistic approach. You can introduce mindfulness practices and emotional regulation techniques to empower students to manage their emotions and make thoughtful choices. For example, starting class with a brief mindfulness exercise can help students center themselves and approach the day with a positive mindset. Focusing on your students' strengths nurtures a positive self-image and reinforces desirable behaviors. Celebrating their individual strengths, like creativity or problem-solving skills, can boost your students' confidence and engagement in learning. When you establish clear behavior expectations and provide consistent feedback, it helps your students understand standards and self-regulate their behavior. Regularly reviewing classroom expectations and acknowledging positive behaviors reinforces desired conduct.

Encourage your students to reflect on their behavior and set goals, as it will foster accountability and ownership. You can have students journal about their actions and discuss their goals for improvement, and watch it encourage their self-awareness and growth. Involving your students in solving behavioral challenges will promote their critical thinking skills. You can also organize group discussions to address class issues as it encourages teamwork and shared responsibility. Teaching empathy is crucial, because it helps your students understand the impact of their actions on others, and it fosters a respectful classroom environment. As you engage your students in activities that promote empathy, such as role-playing scenarios or discussing real-world consequences, it will serve to build their compassion and understanding.

Transitioning to accountability in your classroom requires

acknowledging the personal impact of misbehavior and viewing it as an opportunity for growth and learning. This shift in mindset creates a culture of reflection and consequence comprehension. By combining personal connection with accountability strategies, you can create an environment where students feel supported, valued, and empowered to take ownership of their behavior.

It's natural to feel a personal connection to your students, but it's essential not to internalize disruptive behaviors in a way that compromises your emotional well-being. Constructive redirecting doesn't mean suppressing emotions; rather, it's about maintaining a healthy boundary while addressing misbehavior positively. Viewing disruptions as opportunities for growth and intervention, rather than personal failures, empowers you to navigate challenges with both empathy and accountability.

While it's important for educators to maintain professional boundaries, denying the personal impact of student misbehavior overlooks the genuine care and investment you have in your class's success. By acknowledging this personal connection while also promoting accountability, you can create a more empowering learning environment for all.

Transforming classrooms through the reframing of behaviors is a profound journey that reshapes not just educational methods but also the very essence of our learning spaces. By fostering positive expectations, empathy, and adaptability, you can unlock hidden potentials in students and foster environments that embrace diversity, challenges, and personal growth.

The narrative of Thomas Edison serves as a powerful testament to the lasting impact of positive beliefs and unwavering encouragement in shaping a student's path. Much like Edison's mother, who championed his capabilities and rejected imposed limitations, you can instill a culture of belief, empowerment, and resilience among your students.

Through reframing your classroom's behaviors, you can shift from reactive responses to proactive strategies that address underlying causes of disruptive behaviors. You hold this power to turn challenges into opportunities for learning and development. By embracing diverse learning approaches, empowering students to be active participants in their education, and promoting empathy and understanding, your classroom can become a positive, inclusive space where every student feels valued, supported, and capable of achieving greatness.

6

Fostering Creativity and Innovation

In Renaissance Florence, a young Leonardo da Vinci stood out in his school days not for excelling in traditional subjects, but for his unconventional approach to learning. While his classmates focused on memorizing facts and following the established curriculum, Leonardo's mind was constantly exploring new ideas.

During a lesson on ancient Greek philosophy, Leonardo's teacher asked a question that prompted the class to recite what they had memorized from their textbooks. Leonardo saw this as an opportunity to express his creative insights. Instead of giving the expected response, he shared a narrative that connected the ancient philosophers' ideas to his own innovative thoughts.

This divergence from the norm sometimes led to misunderstandings. Some saw Leonardo's creativity as disruptive, questioning his commitment to formal education. Yet, there were those who recognized the potential in his unconventional thinking, understanding that it could lead to remarkable achievements.

Leonardo's school days were marked by this tension

between conformity and creativity. Despite the challenges, his experiences during this time laid the groundwork for his future as an artist and visionary. His story highlights the importance of nurturing divergent thinking in education, showing that sometimes, the most extraordinary ideas come from those who think outside the box.

Divergent thinking is integral to creative fields such as literature, music, and the like. Writers have to think unconventionally when brainstorming plotlines or developing characters, musicians think differently when composing diverse melodies, and designers must get creative when conceptualizing unique solutions.

Divergent thinking equips individuals with the flexibility to adapt to dynamic challenges and envision novel possibilities. In educational or professional settings, it's essential to embrace unconventional skills to prepare for the complexities of our modern world.

It's time for us to dive deeper into divergent thinking, its characteristics, and its fundamental contrast with convergent thinking. As we delve into subsequent chapters, we will explore practical techniques, its role in various domains, and how individuals can leverage this cognitive process to unlock creativity and innovative problem-solving. Through the lens of divergent thinking, we embark on a journey that transcends traditional boundaries, encouraging creativity and the pursuit of groundbreaking ideas.

Understanding Divergent Thinking and Its Significance

Divergent thinking—a cognitive process characterized by generating unique ideas and solutions in response to an open-ended question—stands in stark contrast to convergent thinking prevalent in traditional education. Convergent thinking, exemplified by seeking a single, correct solution like the mathematical equation $1 + 1 = 2$, emphasizes predetermined answers. The significance of divergent thinking lies in its ability to unleash creativity, encouraging individuals to explore unconventional paths and generate a plethora of ideas, a stark departure from the constraints of convergent thinking. Afterall, how many questions or problems in life have just one absolute answer?

The cognitive flexibility of divergent thinking is crucial in a rapidly evolving world where adaptive problem-solving and innovation are highly valued. In this model, individuals are encouraged to think broadly, allowing for the exploration of various possibilities. This type of thinking is not bound by traditional constraints. Instead, individuals are empowered to break free from pre-established norms and consider unconventional solutions. By fostering a mindset that embraces ambiguity and complexity, divergent thinking becomes a powerful tool for navigating the uncertainties of the modern world.

It also serves as a catalyst for critical thinking, forming a symbiotic relationship between the two cognitive processes. Often underrepresented in traditional education models, critical thinking involves the analysis and synthesis of information. Divergent thinking enhances critical thinking by providing a diverse array of ideas and perspectives that can be evaluated.

Traditional education systems, rooted in convergent thinking, tend to emphasize finding the correct answer to a given problem. This approach limits the development of creative thinking and the exploration of alternative solutions. Divergent thinking, on the other hand, encourages individuals to question assumptions, challenge existing paradigms, and consider alternative viewpoints. This fosters the kind of open-mindedness that is crucial for critical thinking. Just like Leonardo da Vinci, who questioned assumptions and embraced looking at things from a different perspective, educators can encourage students to explore alternative viewpoints which makes way for fresh innovation.

In educational settings, where the emphasis has historically been on convergent thinking, fostering divergent thinking is paramount. Encouraging students to explore various approaches to problem-solving not only nurtures creativity but also equips them with the ability to thoughtfully evaluate information. It challenges the notion that there is only one correct answer and encourages students to navigate the complexities of real-world challenges.

Divergent thinking is also a dynamic cognitive process that challenges the prevailing norms of traditional education. Its original definition, embracing the exploration of diverse and unconventional possibilities, coupled with its ability to break down traditional barriers, foster creativity, and contribute to critical thinking, makes it an invaluable skill in preparing individuals for modern life. The irony lies in the fact that, although we value creativity as a society, we do little to systematically develop it in our schools.

Embracing divergent thinking, therefore, can be the transformative force in steering education toward a more intellectually agile future. By acknowledging its significance and actively incorporating it into educational practices, we can better prepare individuals to thrive in a world that demands not only knowledge but also the ability to think creatively and critically, ultimately contributing to a more innovative society.

The NASA Creativity Study: The Link Between Creativity and Divergent Thinking

The NASA Creativity Study, spearheaded by Dr. George Land and Dr. Beth Jarman in the late 1960s, was a landmark event. Not only did it uncover the intrinsic link between creativity and divergent thinking, but it also ignited the idea to reconsider our educational paradigms. Commissioned by NASA to assess the creative potential of its scientists and engineers within the context of space exploration, the study transcended its initial objectives, yielding insights that reverberate far beyond the confines of space science.

Land and Jarman crafted a special creativity test. Through it, they acknowledged the limitations of conventional measures of intelligence and problem solving and encapsulated the nuanced essence of creativity. The revolutionary new instrument they created aimed to evaluate the unique cognitive ability of divergent thinking among NASA scientists. It was a formal departure from traditional assessments fixated on singular correct answers. Instead, their new test encouraged participants to consider diverse perspectives. It urged them to think beyond the obvious and to emphasize fluency, flexibility, and originality in their responses.

NASA scientists and engineers found themselves immersed in this innovative creativity test, navigating a series of questions meticulously designed to elicit imaginative solutions. Within a limited timeframe, participants not only demonstrated their capacity for divergent thinking but also showcased the richness of their creative abilities, underscoring the multifaceted nature of creativity itself.

The findings of the NASA Creativity Study illuminated a robust correlation between creativity and divergent thinking. Those who excelled in generating a broad array of creative solutions on the test displayed heightened creativity in their professional roles. This correlation effectively challenged established notions of intelligence and problem-solving. It encouraged the recognition and cultivation of divergent thinking skills as pivotal for fostering creativity. This imperative was particularly emphasized in the complex field of space exploration, where innovative solutions are paramount.

Beyond the correlation, the study ventured into intriguing insights into the nature of creative genius. The revelation that 98% of five-year-olds exhibited high levels of divergent thinking—in stark contrast to the mere 2% of adults with similar proficiency—suggested a potential decline in these abilities as individuals transitioned from childhood to adulthood. This observation prompted a critical examination of traditional educational and societal structures, hinting at their possible contribution to the diminishment of divergent thinking skills over time.

The results of the study challenged the prevailing notion that creative genius was an inherent trait possessed by a select few. Instead, it proposed that creative genius was a quality that could be cultivated and potentially rekindled in people over the course of their lives. This implication urged a fundamental reconsideration of educational approaches, emphasizing the need for environments that fostered and sustained divergent thinking throughout various stages of life.

Overall, the NASA Creativity Study, with its emphasis on the integral relationship between creativity and divergent thinking, became a cornerstone for redefining how we cultivate creativity. The insights gleaned from this pioneering study extend beyond the boundaries of space science, resonating profoundly in the field of education.

The implications of divergent thinking require us to recognize and nurture diverse cognitive abilities as they are essential for fostering creativity. This study beckons educators to create environments that not only acknowledge but also celebrate the multifaceted nature of human creativity, fostering a future where innovative thinking flourishes at every stage of life.

Assessing Divergent Thinking in Children: Nurturing Creative Potential

When tailoring creativity tests for children, the paramount consideration is the use of age-appropriate assessment tools. For younger students, tasks involving drawing or storytelling prove effective. For instance, a prompt such as "Imagine and draw a new friend from a different planet" encourages imaginative thinking in young minds. In contrast, older students might engage with more intricate scenarios, such as problem-solving tasks linked to real-world issues or creative writing assignments.

For example, in a science class, students could be challenged to design an eco-friendly city, fostering both divergent thinking and the application of scientific principles. Clear and simple language in instructions ensures accessibility for all students, irrespective of linguistic proficiency.

Seamlessly integrating creativity tests into existing curricula is a practical approach for classroom implementation. In a mathematics class, students could be tasked with solving a problem using multiple approaches, thereby assessing both their mathematical skills and encouraging divergent thinking.

Incorporating technology offers an additional avenue. An online platform presents students with interactive challenges, such as creating a digital story or puzzle. This innovation not only engages students but also provides educators with valuable insights into their creative problem-solving skills.

Identifying creative potential in diverse learning styles is a multifaceted endeavor crucial for fostering innovation and originality in education. Students possess unique strengths, preferences, and ways of processing information. Recognizing and harnessing these differences can unlock untapped creative potential.

In arts and expression, diversity in learning styles is evident. In an art class, some students may excel at visually representing ideas through drawing or painting, while others might prefer expressing themselves through written or spoken words. Providing a variety of mediums and encouraging exploration allows educators to identify and nurture creative potential in students with different artistic inclinations.

Beyond the arts, diverse learning styles also manifest in problem-solving approaches. In science or math classes, for instance, some students may gravitate towards logical and analytical methods while others thrive in more hands-on, experiential learning. Creating a learning environment that accommodates both systematic thinkers and those who learn best through practical application ensures that creative potential is identified and developed across a spectrum of learning styles.

Additionally, technology integration plays a crucial role in recognizing diverse learning styles. Interactive platforms, educational apps, and multimedia resources cater to students who thrive in digitally immersive environments. By incorporating technology, educators can identify creative potential in students who excel in navigating digital tools.

Moreover, assessing creative potential involves understanding how students engage with information beyond traditional metrics. Some students may excel in collaborative group settings, while others may thrive in independent study. By recognizing these preferences, educators can tailor teaching methods to ensure that each student's unique creative capacities are identified and nurtured.

Identifying creative potential in diverse learning styles requires a nuanced and inclusive approach. By offering a range of opportunities for expression, problem-solving, and utilizing technology while considering various engagement preferences, educators can uncover and nurture the distinct creative capacities within each student. This approach not only enhances the learning experience but also contributes to a more innovative and adaptable generation prepared to navigate the complexities of the modern world.

Integrating Divergent Thinking Into the Curriculum

Integrating divergent thinking into your curriculum is not just a trend but a crucial strategy for fostering creativity, critical thinking, and problem-solving skills among students. It equips them for success in the 21st century. Let's delve deeper into practical strategies that seamlessly incorporate divergent thinking across subjects, promote collaboration through effective brainstorming techniques, leverage technology for creative exploration, and provide detailed examples to guide your implementation efforts.

One of the fundamental pillars of divergent thinking is fostering collaboration and brainstorming sessions among your students. Group activities offer fertile ground for generating fresh ideas while also providing diverse perspectives. For instance, consider organizing a project in your science class where students collaborate to design an experiment that explores the real-world application of a scientific concept. This not only encourages innovative approaches but also instills invaluable problem-solving skills. Similarly, you can challenge your biology class to develop a collaborative experiment investigating the impact of different environmental factors on plant growth, fostering a deeper understanding of ecological dynamics.

To effectively facilitate brainstorming sessions, employ techniques like mind mapping or free association exercises. These methods help guide discussions, foster open-mindedness, and create a safe space for expression. They ignite students' creativity and encourage them to explore unconventional solutions. In a language arts class, for example, conducting a brainstorming session to generate creative ideas for a collaborative storytelling project can be highly engaging. Introduce thought-provoking prompts to spark the imagination and encourage students to contribute unique plot twists and character developments.

As you can see, divergent thinking seamlessly integrates into various subjects, offering a holistic approach to education that nurtures multifaceted skills. In science, introduce open-ended experiments that encourage creative problem-solving and promote scientific inquiry and imaginative thinking. For instance, challenge students to design an eco-friendly solution to a real-world environmental issue. This can push them to think critically about sustainability and innovation. Similarly, in math, you could present real-world problems that require innovative approaches and different problem-solving strategies, such as budgeting for a community project, which enhances mathematical skills while fostering divergent thinking. Language arts classes can provide fertile ground for divergent thinking activities through collaborative storytelling or creative writing workshops. These activities stimulate students' imaginations, encourage them to think outside the box, and promote the development of unique narrative styles.

Interdisciplinary approaches further enhance divergent thinking by connecting concepts across multiple subjects. For example, collaborating between science and art classes to visually represent scientific principles through creative projects helps students master both subjects. It not only reinforces scientific concepts but also fosters artistic expression and critical thinking.

Technology offers a powerful platform for fostering divergent thinking by providing digital tools that facilitate creative exploration and expression. Consider using virtual brainstorming platforms for real-time idea contributions and collaborative online platforms for asynchronous collaboration. This can enable students to engage in creative dialogue beyond the confines of their physical classroom. However, it's essential to strike a balance between screen time and hands-on activities to ensure a well-rounded learning experience.

Incorporating physical materials and activities into lessons can enhance creativity by engaging multiple senses and promoting kinesthetic learning. For example, students can use digital resources to research and plan a project and then transition to hands-on implementation and presentation, combining the benefits of technology with tactile experiences. This approach not only enriches learning but also caters to different learning styles, ensuring that all students can thrive in a divergent thinking environment.

In conclusion, integrating divergent thinking into your

curriculum is a transformative approach that nurtures students' creativity, critical thinking, and problem-solving skills. By encouraging collaboration, incorporating divergent thinking across subjects, leveraging technology judiciously, and providing hands-on learning experiences, you can create a dynamic learning environment that equips your students with essential skills for success. Through effective implementation of divergent thinking strategies, you can empower your students to become innovative thinkers ready to tackle the complexities and challenges of the modern era.

Divergent Thinking in Assessment and Evaluation: A Paradigm Shift Towards Authenticity

The recognition of divergent thinking as a key skill in education necessitates a fundamental reevaluation of assessment and evaluation methods. Traditional assessment methods, often centered around convergent thinking and standardized testing, may not fully capture the authentic depth of students' abilities, strengths, and talents. Consider how, in traditional grading, assignments and assessments can be perceived as mere checkpoints for grades, quickly forgotten and deemed as busywork. This unfortunate reality often leads to many creative and dedicated efforts by students being overlooked and undervalued. Perhaps worst of all, it leaves them questioning the significance of their work.

On the other hand, incorporating divergent thinking into assessment practices not only acknowledges individual uniqueness but also cultivates a more authentic representation of student capabilities.

Imagine a scenario where you, as an educator, are evaluating a student's work. Instead of relying solely on traditional grading methods, you could consider the power of portfolio assessment. A collection of diverse artifacts, ranging from essays to artistic creations and problem-solving projects, can paint a rich tapestry that reflects the multifaceted nature of divergent thinking. Portfolios not only showcase correct answers but also the iterative process, experimentation, and evolving thought patterns of students. This approach allows you to witness the intellectual journey unfolding before your eyes, providing a dynamic snapshot of each student's growth and creativity over time.

Contrast this with standardized testing, which often reduces students to numerical scores. Alternative measures, such as real-world simulations and project-based assessments, offer authenticity by mimicking genuine problem-solving scenarios. These assessments shed light on practical skills like critical thinking and adaptability, which are crucial in professional settings. The authenticity of these measures lies in their ability to evaluate not just theoretical knowledge but also its application in real and complex situations.

One common concern among educators is the perceived time-consuming nature of offering feedback. It's essential to emphasize that authentic feedback need not be an arduous process. Instead, it plays a pivotal role in the assessment process, contributing to a holistic understanding of each student's capabilities without significantly increasing your time commitments.

Consider how you can provide feedback on a student's writing assignment. Rather than spending hours crafting detailed feedback, you could focus on highlighting the student's strong points, such as insightful analysis or creative storytelling techniques. This positive reinforcement acknowledges the student's unique strengths and talents, instantly boosting their confidence and motivation to continue improving. Additionally, provide brief yet impactful personalized feedback, pointing out areas for further development, like refining arguments or using evidence effectively. This tailored guidance offers specific insights into how students can leverage their strengths for continued growth.

You have the power to create an authentic dialogue that fosters a supportive learning environment by balancing positive reinforcement with targeted feedback. This approach capitalizes on the role of feedback in guiding students toward success while respecting your time constraints as an educator.

In other words, embracing divergent thinking in assessment and evaluation opens doors to authenticity, allowing you to recognize and nurture the diverse capabilities and talents of each student effectively.

Showcasing Authentic Student Work

There is a unique opportunity to shift the paradigm by actively highlighting and celebrating the individuality and creativity of each student. By creating platforms that do that, you can infuse a renewed sense of meaning and value into their contributions. In doing so, you not only counteract the dismissiveness associated with traditional assignments but also foster an environment where students recognize the inherent worth of their efforts, paving the way for a more authentic and enriching learning experience.

Consider developing a digital showcase where students can proudly display their creations. Not only would this preserve their efforts, but it would provide a lasting and meaningful representation of their accomplishments, ensuring their work is seen and valued beyond the classroom. Likewise, you could encourage students to present their work to peers as well, fostering an environment where their efforts are acknowledged and celebrated. This not only addresses the issue of work being discarded but also enhances public speaking skills and promotes collaboration among students.

Furthermore, connecting student projects with the community can have a profound impact. Whether through exhibitions, partnerships with local organizations, or presentations to parents, involving the community creates a sense of purpose and impact beyond the classroom. That's when students see that their work has a meaningful place in the broader context, dispelling any sense of disposability and reinforcing the value of their contributions.

Highlighting the individuality of student work becomes a key aspect of shifting away from the dismissiveness of traditional assignments. Creating a culture that actively appreciates and celebrates each student's unique contributions counters the feeling of insignificance. By embracing and spotlighting individuality, you ensure that no work is treated as "discarded work," fostering an environment where every student feels valued and their efforts are recognized.

By addressing the potential problems of traditional work and showcasing your students' authentic contributions, you as an educator can instill a sense of pride and purpose in students' academic endeavors. This not only bolsters the authenticity of the learning experience but also reinforces the idea that each student's unique abilities and talents are integral to the overall educational journey.

Additionally, integrating student work into interdisciplinary projects can further amplify the impact, allowing students to see the relevance of their work across various subjects and real-world contexts. This interconnected approach not only enhances student engagement but also fosters a deeper understanding of the interconnectedness of knowledge and skills. Through these collaborative efforts, students develop critical thinking, communication, and problem-solving skills essential for success in the 21st century.

Empowering the Creative Potential in Every Child

Revisiting the crucial connection between creativity and education, the NASA Creativity Study was a landmark, challenging conventional ideas and urging a transformative shift in educational paradigms. This exploration unveils stories that exemplify the profound impact of early encouragement, with Walt Disney's journey serving as a compelling narrative. Disney's fond memories often included his seventh-grade teacher, Miss Daisy Beck, who played a pivotal role in recognizing and nurturing his artistic talents, which laid the foundation for a lifetime of creative achievements.

Miss Daisy Beck's influence on Walt Disney goes beyond the personal; it shaped the very fabric of our cultural landscape. Could you imagine a world without the impact of Walt Disney? The enchantment of animated classics, the magic of Disneyland, and the creativity that has touched generations worldwide—all bear the indelible mark of a teacher who recognized and nurtured a young boy's creative spark.

In reflecting on Disney's story, one can't help but ponder how many potential visionaries, innovators, and future Disneys are missing out because they aren't encouraged in the way Miss Beck encouraged him. The transformative power of early encouragement cannot be overstated. It doesn't just shape individual destinies but influences the cultural fabric of our society.

Considering such revelations, we are presented with a compelling call to action. The intricate nature of human creativity necessitates the creation of environments that celebrate diverse cognitive abilities. Parents are key partners in fostering creative expression at home, while policymakers bear the responsibility of reimagining educational systems to accommodate the unique needs of highly creative individuals.

A fundamental aspect of nurturing highly creative students involves a nuanced approach to identification and support. Traditional measures like standardized testing fall short in capturing the intricate dimensions of creative potential. Instead, educators will need to adopt a comprehensive evaluation strategy that goes beyond conventional assessments. Being attuned to indicators such as unconventional problem-solving, a propensity for diverse perspectives, and a passion for innovation is crucial in identifying highly creative students.

Supporting these students goes beyond acknowledging their creative tendencies. It requires fostering an environment that encourages and nourishes their unique perspectives. Educators must be prepared to adapt their teaching methods to accommodate the unconventional approaches that highly creative students often employ. By recognizing and understanding the distinct needs of these students, teachers can provide tailored support that allows their creativity to flourish.

Encouraging collaboration is another essential element in nurturing highly creative students. Collaborative projects and group activities provide platforms for students to share and build upon each other's ideas, fostering a culture of innovation. Integrating real-world problem-solving scenarios into the curriculum provides practical outlets for creative expression, linking classroom learning to tangible applications.

Walt Disney's early experiences, especially his fond recollections of Miss Daisy Beck's influence, serve as a poignant example of the transformative impact educators can have on highly creative individuals. The classroom, as a creative incubator, played a crucial role in Disney's development, emphasizing the significance of educational environments in fostering creative genius. Similarly, stories like Leonardo da Vinci's showcase the timeless impact of early encouragement on creative brilliance.

In conclusion, nurturing highly creative students demands a departure from traditional educational approaches. The NASA Creativity Study, with its revelation of the integral link between creativity and divergent thinking, serves as a guidepost for this transformative journey. By drawing inspiration from stories like Walt Disney's and Leonardo da Vinci's and actively incorporating insights from such studies, educators can create environments that not only acknowledge but also celebrate the diverse and boundless nature of human creativity.

You can embrace a holistic educational approach that fosters innovation and unlocks the full spectrum of creative potential within every highly creative student that comes through your door. Through such efforts, you can contribute not only to the development of future visionaries but also to a society where innovative thinking flourishes at every stage of life.

7

Creating a Positive Classroom Environment: Strategies for Effective Classroom Management

Classroom management is the backbone of a successful learning environment. It refers to the strategies and techniques used by teachers to establish a structured and organized classroom where students can thrive academically and socially. Effective classroom management ensures that students are engaged, focused, and on task, allowing the teacher to deliver quality instruction and facilitate meaningful learning experiences.

One key element of classroom management is establishing clear rules and expectations. By setting guidelines for behavior and academic performance, teachers can provide students with a framework for success. These rules need to be communicated effectively to ensure that students understand what is expected of them. Additionally, teachers must consistently enforce these rules to maintain a positive learning environment.

Another important aspect of classroom management is building relationships with students. When students feel valued and respected, they are more likely to be engaged and motivated to learn. Teachers can create a sense of community by getting to know their students on a personal level, showing genuine interest in their lives and well-being. This fosters a positive and supportive learning environment where students feel comfortable taking risks and asking for help when needed.

Setting High Expectations in the Classroom

Creating a positive learning environment is a cornerstone of effective teaching. It begins with setting high expectations for your students and understanding the impact of your beliefs and actions, including the Pygmalion Effect discussed earlier. When you believe in their potential and hold them to high standards, students are more likely to rise to meet those expectations. High expectations not only challenge students academically but also encourage them to be respectful, responsible, and engaged in their learning journey.

By setting high expectations, you will send a clear message to your students that you believe in their abilities and value their education. Your belief will motivate students to take ownership of their learning and strive for success. Additionally, high expectations can help create a culture of excellence in your classroom, where students inspire and motivate each other to do their best.

To set high expectations effectively, start by communicating clearly with your students about behavior, effort, and academic achievement from the first day of class. Use straightforward language that eliminates confusion and helps students understand what is expected of them. Encourage active participation from students in establishing class expectations. It will foster a sense of ownership and responsibility among them.

Furthermore, frame your expectations positively to promote desired behaviors and cultivate a growth mindset. Instead of focusing on what students shouldn't do, emphasize what they should do. For example, instead of saying, "Don't interrupt others," you can say, "Wait for your turn to speak." This positive framing encourages students to focus on desired behaviors and fosters a sense of empowerment.

Consistency is crucial in maintaining these expectations across all students, ensuring fairness and clarity. Be consistent in enforcing expectations and providing support and guidance to help students meet them. Celebrate their successes and encourage them to keep pushing themselves to reach even higher.

Another key aspect of setting high expectations is involving students in the process. Encourage active participation from students in shaping the rules and guidelines for behavior for the classroom. This collaborative approach not only enhances student engagement but also promotes a shared commitment to maintaining a positive classroom environment.

Modeling the behaviors you expect from your students is also essential. As their teacher, you serve as a role model, and your actions speak louder than words. Demonstrate the expected behaviors consistently, as your actions serve as powerful examples for students to emulate. For instance, if punctuality is emphasized, ensure you are consistently on time for class.

Incorporating these strategies into your classroom management approach will lay a strong foundation for a positive and structured learning environment. This environment encourages collaboration, mutual respect, and a genuine enthusiasm for learning among students. Students are more likely to take ownership of their learning when they feel that their teacher has confidence in them and values their education.

Ultimately, setting high expectations empowers students to reach their full potential and achieve academic excellence. It creates a culture where students are inspired to excel, support each other, and embrace challenges as opportunities for growth. This positive learning environment not only benefits students academically but also nurtures their personal and social development, preparing them for success in the classroom and beyond.

The Power of Classroom Routines: Fostering a Positive Learning Environment

Establishing a positive learning environment in the classroom is greatly enhanced using routines, which provide a structured framework that helps students feel secure and focused on learning. They create predictability and organization, allowing students to understand what to expect and reducing distractions related to classroom logistics. Moreover, routines are more important than rules because they teach students what they should be doing, rather than focusing solely on what they shouldn't be doing.

One of the key benefits of incorporating student responsibilities into routines is the development of a sense of ownership and accountability. For example, a morning routine could include designated students responsible for passing out materials, checking homework assignments, or setting up classroom displays. These responsibilities not only help streamline classroom activities but also foster a sense of pride and importance in students' contributions to the learning environment.

By establishing clear routines that include student responsibilities, you can create a culture of collaboration and teamwork where students learn to rely on each other and work together towards common goals. This collaborative approach not only benefits academic tasks but also promotes social and emotional growth by encouraging empathy, cooperation, and mutual support among students.

Furthermore, routines with student responsibilities can contribute to a sense of agency for your class. When you entrust your students with meaningful tasks, they will feel valued and motivated to actively engage in classroom activities. That's because a sense of agency will boost their confidence, encourage them to take initiative, and foster a positive attitude towards learning.

Consistent routines with student responsibilities also play a crucial role in promoting positive behavior and classroom management. When students understand their roles and responsibilities, they are more likely to exhibit respectful and cooperative behaviors. Routines help establish clear expectations, reduce disruptions, and create a harmonious learning environment where students feel safe, respected, and supported.

Additionally, routines that involve student responsibilities support the development of essential life skills such as leadership, time management, and teamwork. As students take on various tasks within the classroom, they learn how to manage their responsibilities effectively, collaborate with peers, and problem-solve in real-time situations. These skills are invaluable for their academic success and future endeavors.

Moreover, incorporating student responsibilities into classroom routines is a powerful strategy for fostering a positive and productive learning environment. These routines not only provide structure and organization but also empower students, promote collaboration, and develop essential life skills. By implementing clear and consistent routines with student responsibilities, you can create a dynamic and inclusive classroom where your students thrive academically, socially, and emotionally.

Creating Seamless Transitions: The Power of Music in Lower Grades

Establishing smooth transitions between activities is crucial for maintaining an organized and focused classroom environment, particularly in lower grades where attention spans can be shorter. One effective and engaging strategy to signal transitions is the use of music. By serving as a pleasant auditory cue, music adds an element of fun and excitement to the learning experience.

When planning transitions, it's important to consider the grade level of your students. Depending on the grade level, you may begin by incorporating a consistent daily schedule that includes designated time slots for different subjects and activities. A predictable routine provides a foundation for effective transitions. Instead of verbally announcing transitions, consider using music as a non-verbal cue. Playing a specific song or tune during transitions between subjects or activities can help students seamlessly transition without the need for verbal prompts. The choice of music can be thematic or simply a cheerful melody that signals a shift in focus. This approach allows students to associate the music with the upcoming transition, making the process more intuitive.

Another aspect to consider is the classroom layout. Ensure that your classroom layout supports the flow of activities. You will need to designate specific areas for different types of learning and organize materials to minimize transition time. An organized layout, combined with music, can create a seamless transition experience for students. Additionally, incorporating visual cues along with music can enhance transitions. Displaying a visual schedule or a countdown timer in a designated area visible to students can help them anticipate and understand upcoming transitions better.

Maintaining flexibility within the routine is also key.

Consider making transitions enjoyable by using themed music or sound effects to match the subject or activity. For example, using a calming melody for quiet reading time and a lively tune for energetic activities can make transitions more engaging for students. Fun elements will capture your students' attention and contribute to a positive classroom environment.

Remember, using music as a transitional tool in lower grades can streamline activity flow and add creativity and joy to your classroom. By considering the grade level of your students, planning consistent schedules, utilizing both verbal and visual cues, and maintaining flexibility, you can create a positive and structured learning environment that supports smooth transitions between activities. Once your students know what to do, it will be important to have a few rules in place to help them understand what is and is not allowed.

Establishing Clear and Effective Classroom Rules

Establishing clear and effective classroom rules is crucial for fostering a positive learning environment. While expectations and routines should be the primary focus of the class, it's important to recognize the necessity of rules in helping to establish boundaries, order, respect, and other essential aspects of classroom management. Rules provide needed boundaries and guidelines, which can contribute to maintaining order and promoting respect and cooperation among students.

When establishing rules, it's helpful to involve your students in the process. Discuss with them the importance of rules and why they are necessary for creating a positive learning environment. Brainstorm together what the rules should be and come up with a set of rules that are fair, reasonable, and relevant to the needs of the classroom. Make sure the rules are clearly communicated, posted in the classroom, and consistently enforced.

When students understand and follow the rules, they can feel safe and secure in the classroom. They know what is expected of them and what the consequences will be if they choose to break the rules. These clear expectations will allow them to focus on learning and interact with their peers in a positive and respectful manner.

Creating a conducive learning environment involves the establishment of clear and reasonable rules. Keep the rules simple, limiting them to a manageable amount that students can easily remember and adhere to. Make sure to clearly communicate the consequences of not following the established rules, making sure they are fair and logically connected to the rule violation. Next, you'll need to implement a system of positive reinforcement to encourage adherence to the rules. You could try verbal praise, tangible rewards, or acknowledgment in front of peers. Each student may respond better to different positive reactions since all your students are unique.

Make sure to regularly review the rules with your students to reinforce their understanding and adherence. This reflective process not only informs students about their behavior but can also allow you to adapt rules to the evolving dynamics of your classroom. While posting rules may vary in its necessity based on the age of your students and your classroom's dynamics, it can serve as a visual reinforcement of expectations and aid in comprehension, especially for younger students or those with specific learning needs.

E

stablishing clear and effective classroom rules is essential for creating a positive and productive learning environment. By involving your students in the rule-making process, providing clear communication and consequences, implementing positive reinforcement, and regularly reviewing and reflecting on the rules, you can foster a classroom culture that promotes respect, cooperation, and active engagement in learning.

Organizing the Physical Classroom Space

A well-organized physical classroom space plays a crucial role in shaping your class's learning experience, setting the stage for effective instruction and influencing your engagement, interaction, and overall academic success. Optimizing the classroom layout and utilizing resources effectively are essential components of creating an environment that fosters learning and growth.

Various design principles can be employed to arrange desks and instructional areas in a way that promotes interaction, collaboration, and flexibility. For instance, creating clusters of desks instead of traditional rows facilitates group work and peer-to-peer learning. Likewise, strategically placing instructional areas such as reading corners, science nooks, and art stations encourages exploration and hands-on learning.

The physical arrangement of the classroom significantly impacts your engagement. Creating designated spaces for different activities can signal your expectations to your class, helping you transition between tasks effectively and stay engaged throughout the day.

In today's digital age, technology plays a pivotal role in education. Incorporating interactive whiteboards, educational software, and multimedia resources enriches lessons and caters to diverse learning styles. Visual aids, such as educational posters, infographics, and charts, also serve as powerful tools for reinforcing concepts and promoting visual learning.

Creating a resource-rich environment involves strategically organizing learning materials, manipulatives, and reference books, allowing you to access resources independently and empowering you to explore topics of interest. Furthermore, incorporating tactile and kinesthetic resources, such as building blocks, art supplies, and hands-on learning kits, accommodates diverse learning styles and supports experiential learning.

Recognizing and accommodating your individual needs within the physical space is paramount in creating an inclusive and supportive learning environment. As an example, allowing students the choice to sit where they want, whether on the floor, by their desks, or in a preferred position, reflects your commitment to creating an environment that suits your students' individual needs. You'll find it also enhances engagement as children are more likely to participate when they have a choice in something.

You can designate areas for quiet reflection, collaborative work, and hands-on exploration. Having these separate areas assists the diverse ways in which students engage with content and express their understanding.

Creativity, adaptability, and willingness to innovate are the keys to transforming your classroom into a vibrant hub of learning. Through continual reflection and refinement of classroom organization and resource utilization, you can ensure that students have an environment that not only meets their educational needs but also nurtures their intellectual curiosity and love for learning. In essence, the physical classroom space becomes an extension of our educational philosophy and a manifestation of our commitment to providing the best possible learning experiences for the next generation.

The Role of Rewards and Consequences in Shaping Behavior

Rewards and consequences play vital roles in behavior management within the classroom, significantly influencing behavior and contributing to a positive learning atmosphere. Effectively utilizing rewards and consequences will enable you to motivate students, reinforce positive behaviors, address misbehavior, and guide your class towards responsible decision-making.

Rewards act as potent incentives that encourage students to exhibit desirable behaviors and achieve academic success. These incentives can manifest in various forms, such as verbal praise, certificates, privileges, or tokens of recognition. It is essential for rewards to hold meaning and align with the classroom's goals and expectations. For example, acknowledging a student's effort in completing a challenging assignment not only recognizes their hard work but also reinforces the value of perseverance and diligence. Similarly, awarding a certificate for exemplary behavior reinforces positive classroom norms, encouraging students to continue displaying respectful and cooperative behaviors. You will likely find which rewards work best for your particular students.

Conversely, consequences are designed to address misbehavior and provide students with opportunities for reflection and growth. It's important to note that correct consequences are fair, consistent, and directly related to the specific misbehavior. For instance, if a student disrupts a class discussion, an appropriate consequence might involve a brief time-out for self-reflection and a discussion on improving behavior. The aim is to use consequences as teaching tools rather than punitive measures, guiding students towards understanding the consequences of their actions and facilitating positive changes.

Incorporating real-life examples into the learning process reinforces desired behaviors and discourages undesirable ones. For instance, a student who actively participates in class discussions and demonstrates good listening skills could be rewarded with leading a group activity. This would not only acknowledge their positive contributions but would also motivate them to continue engaging in classroom activities. Conversely, if a student engages in disruptive behavior during group work, a consequence like temporarily losing a privilege related to group activities would emphasize the importance of respectful collaboration.

Furthermore, consistent application of rewards and consequences establishes clear expectations and boundaries in the classroom. When students understand that positive behaviors receive recognition and negative behaviors have consequences, they are more likely to make thoughtful choices aligned with classroom standards. This fosters a sense of accountability and empowers students to take responsibility for their actions and their impact on the learning environment.

It's worth noting that natural rewards and consequences are fundamental aspects of life, even for adults. In professional environments, employees receive recognition for their contributions through promotions, bonuses, or public acknowledgment. On the other hand, there are consequences for not meeting expectations or violating company policies. Similarly, students benefit from understanding this balance in the educational setting, as it prepares them for future responsibilities and accountability.

In summary, rewards and consequences serve as essential tools for shaping behavior and maintaining a positive classroom climate. When implemented strategically and consistently, they not only motivate students to exhibit desired behaviors but also provide valuable learning experiences that promote responsibility, accountability, and self-regulation. By integrating examples and fostering a supportive environment, you can effectively leverage rewards and consequences to create a classroom culture conducive to learning, growth, and positive social interactions.

Dealing With Challenging Behavior: Strategies for Success

Dealing with challenging behavior in the classroom requires a multifaceted approach, especially when persistent misbehavior calls for alternative strategies. When addressing challenging behavior, it's crucial to adopt an empathetic stance, understand the student's perspective, and focus on finding solutions rather than assigning blame.

One effective approach is to foster a positive relationship with the student. This involves investing time and effort in getting to know them on a personal level, identifying their strengths and weaknesses, and building a rapport based on empathy and respect. Building a positive relationship not only helps in understanding the underlying causes of the behavior but also creates a supportive and safe environment where the student feels valued, understood, and more willing to engage constructively.

Another valuable strategy involves using positive reinforcement to encourage desired behavior. Positive reinforcement entails acknowledging and praising the student for demonstrating positive actions and behaviors. This can be in the form of verbal praise, acknowledgment in front of peers, certificates, privileges, or other meaningful rewards. Positive reinforcement not only reinforces the desired behavior but also boosts the student's self-esteem, self-confidence, and motivation to continue making positive choices.

In cases where challenging behavior persists despite initial interventions, implementing a behavior plan may be necessary. A behavior plan is a structured approach that outlines clear expectations for behavior, consequences for misbehavior, and any additional support or interventions required to address the underlying issues. It is crucial to involve the student in the development of the behavior plan to ensure their understanding, ownership, and commitment to the agreed-upon expectations and consequences. Additionally, collaborating with parents or guardians can provide valuable insights and support in implementing the behavior plan consistently across different environments.

Additionally, incorporating restorative practices can be beneficial in addressing challenging behavior and fostering a positive classroom environment. Restorative practices focus on repairing harm, restoring relationships, and promoting mutual respect. Restorative conversations provide a platform for students to reflect on their actions, take responsibility, understand the impact of their behavior on others, and work towards making amends. This approach encourages empathy, communication, problem-solving skills, and conflict resolution, contributing to a more cohesive and harmonious classroom community.

For instance, consider a scenario where a student consistently disrupts your class by speaking out of turn and not following instructions. Instead of immediately resorting to disciplinary measures, you arrange a restorative conversation with the student. During this conversation, you and your student discuss the impact of the behavior on the class's learning environment, explore the reasons behind the behavior, and collaboratively devise a plan to address it. The plan may include setting specific behavioral goals, establishing regular check-ins to monitor progress, providing positive reinforcement for demonstrating desired behaviors, and implementing consequences for repeated misbehavior.

Implementing a behavior contract can also be an effective strategy for addressing persistent challenging behavior. A behavior contract is a written agreement between your student, you, the teacher, and possibly parents or guardians that clearly outlines behavior expectations, consequences for misbehavior, and rewards for demonstrating positive behaviors. The contract should be specific, measurable, achievable, relevant, and time-bound (SMART) to ensure clarity and accountability in behavior management. Regular reviews and revisions of the behavior contract can allow for ongoing monitoring, adjustment, and reinforcement of desired behaviors.

By combining relationship-building, positive reinforcement, behavior plans, restorative practices, and behavior contracts, you can create a tailored approach to managing and addressing challenging behavior effectively. These strategies not only address the immediate behavior concerns but also contribute to creating a positive, inclusive, and conducive learning environment where all students can thrive academically, socially, and emotionally.

The Impact of a Positive Learning Environment on Student Achievement

A positive learning environment exerts a profound influence on student achievement, fostering an atmosphere where students feel secure, valued, and encouraged to excel. This environment cultivates active engagement, risk-taking, and resilience in the face of challenges.

Within such a setting, students feel empowered to ask questions, seek assistance, and actively participate in class activities. They take ownership of their learning journey, setting ambitious goals and channeling increased motivation and effort towards their academic pursuits. This, of course, results in elevated levels of accomplishment.

A positive learning environment nurtures teacher-student relationships, reinforcing a sense of connection, care, and support. Students who perceive their teachers as invested in their success exhibit higher levels of engagement and dedication to their studies. This rapport fosters mutual trust, respect, and collaboration among peers, leading to a cohesive and supportive classroom community.

Extensive research corroborates the correlation between a positive learning environment and enhanced academic performance, improved conduct, and heightened student engagement. This means that by curating such an environment, you wield significant influence over your students' academic progress and overall well-being.

Don't forget. The integral facets of constructing a positive learning environment include: establishing high expectations, implementing structured routines, delineating clear guidelines, facilitating seamless transitions, utilizing rewards and consequences effectively, and employing strategies to address challenging behavior. When you uphold rigorous standards while providing robust support and guidance, you will empower students to unlock their full potential.

A positive learning environment not only propels academic success but also imparts invaluable life skills such as accountability, self-discipline, and resilience. It instills a passion for learning and a commitment to continual improvement, equipping students with the tools they need to thrive both academically and personally.

8

The Impact of Recess, Play, and Brain Breaks on Student Behavior and Achievement

In my experience teaching life science, I discovered a powerful strategy that transformed how I approached classroom management. I created a space in the back of the room where students could go to reset. For instance, I had a student with ADHD who would get fidgety during class. Instead of traditional disciplinary measures, I allowed him to do pushups for 2 or 3 minutes in the back of the class. Surprisingly, this simple solution helped him refocus and stay engaged in learning.

This approach not only worked wonders for that student but also caught the attention of his father and other teachers. His father, impressed by the positive change, asked me why his son never got in trouble in my class. I shared with him the strategy of allowing physical activity as a reset, and he immediately asked other teachers if the same could be implemented in their classes.

Now, some thought it might be disruptive at first. However, I found that after the initial adjustment period, it became the norm, and other students barely noticed it at all. Moreover, it was much less distracting than the disruptive behaviors the student exhibited when he couldn't stay still.

This experience taught me a valuable lesson about the power of integrating play and physical activity in the classroom for effective classroom management and student engagement.

Harvard psychiatrist John Ratey echoes this sentiment with his belief that the brain and the body are not separate entities; instead, they form a dynamic and interconnected system, emphasizing the transformative impact of physical activity on cognitive function and mental well-being (Ratey, 2008). This concept is at the core of our exploration — the brain-body connection is not just a theoretical construct but a practical reality that can revolutionize education.

Let's take a moment to visualize a classroom atmosphere where traditional disciplinary methods seamlessly coexist with the spontaneity of play, fostering a positive environment conducive to learning. Imagine how this dynamic setup allows students to actively engage with rules, aligning with their natural need for movement and exploration, thereby enhancing the brain-body connection. Not only do the students require less consequences, but they also actually want to participate!

The reason is simple. Incorporating play, recess, and physical activity isn't just about adding fun to the classroom; it's about providing the essential nutrients for student growth and success. It's akin to how "Miracle-Gro" fuels plant development. This approach not only enhances learning but also nurtures resilience, fosters joy in learning, and sets the stage for lifelong success.

As we delve into this dynamic integration, a central theme emerges. It effectively addresses common challenges faced by educators. Disruptive behavior finds an outlet in the joyful abandon of play. Recognizing and incorporating these outlets can transform behavioral issues, resulting in a more focused and engaged student body.

Beyond immediate behavioral impacts, this chapter examines how recess and play provide crucial outlets for stress release. In today's educational landscape, where pressures abound, the integration of play offers students moments of respite, enabling them to recharge and return to the classroom with enhanced focus and a positive mindset.

Additionally, we'll explore the cognitive benefits derived from incorporating physical activity into learning. Once we recognize the connections between movement and cognitive development, it becomes evident that a sedentary approach may hinder intellectual capacities. By prioritizing physical activity, educators can cultivate healthy bodies and agile minds, echoing Ratey's assertion that exercise is the "Miracle-Gro" for the brain.

It's also essential to recognize that often, students who have the hardest time focusing, sitting still, and behaving are the ones who need recess and physical activity the most. This realization aligns with the core premise of the chapter, challenging the traditional separation of structured learning and unstructured play.

That's why it's crucial to explore specific strategies and practical implementations of an educational environment where recess, play, and physical activity become indispensable elements of effective classroom management. It's all grounded in the intricate and essential brain-body connection.

The Importance of Recess, Play, and Brain Breaks in Schools

Research has shown that allowing students regular opportunities for unstructured play and physical activity not only improves their overall well-being but also positively impacts their behavior and academic performance. By allowing children to engage in active play or take short breaks to refresh their minds, teachers can create atmospheres that promote focus, attentiveness, and creativity.

While it was many years ago, I can still remember the joy of recess as a child. I was always watching the clock as it counted down to play time. We had to line up and walk quietly in the hallway, but once outside, it was a race to the kickball field or swings, or whatever I had decided to do while sitting in class waiting. This happened multiple times each day and we even had extended play time during lunch, where I would inhale my lunch quickly so that I could rush to the playground. I made good grades and was an excellent student academically, but this was my favorite part of the school day. In fact, if it weren't for play time, I would not have been able to focus and do as well academically.

I am forever grateful for a principal and teachers who knew the importance of play. It was not a break from learning, but was an integral part of learning, and definitely one of the most enjoyable aspects of school, especially for me. Play—after all—is how children learn.

Not only does playtime provide a much-needed physical outlet, but it also enhances cognitive skills, problem-solving abilities, and social development. Furthermore, brain breaks – short mental or physical activities – have been found to re-energize students, helping them stay engaged and ready to learn.

By recognizing the importance of recess, play, and brain breaks, educators can create an environment that fosters positive behavior, boosts academic achievement, and cultivates well-rounded students. So let's explore how these simple yet powerful strategies can transform the classroom experience and set students up for long-term success.

Play holds a crucial role in shaping student behavior and academic performance. When they are given the opportunity to engage in unstructured activities, students develop essential social and emotional skills. They learn how to negotiate, cooperate, and resolve conflicts, which are essential life skills that contribute to positive behavior in the classroom.

Moreover, research has shown that regular breaks help increase blood flow to the brain, promoting cognitive function and enhancing memory and learning abilities. Additionally, it provides a much-needed opportunity for students to recharge their energy levels, preventing fatigue and improving overall academic performance.

Play is not just a frivolous activity; it is a fundamental aspect of childhood development. When students engage in play, they are actively constructing knowledge, exploring their interests, and developing critical thinking skills. In short, they are growing their brain.

Children can experiment, problem-solve, and think creatively. They learn to take risks, make decisions, and adapt to various situations. Play allows students to practice and apply what they have learned in a hands-on and meaningful way, making their learning experiences more authentic and memorable.

Furthermore, play promotes curiosity and motivation. When students are excited and engaged in their education, they are more likely to retain information and develop a love for learning. By incorporating play-based activities into the curriculum, educators can create a positive and enriching learning environment that fosters student growth and academic success.

In addition, brain breaks are another effective strategy for improving student behavior and achievement in the classroom. They are short mental or physical activities that provide students with a quick pause from academic tasks, allowing them to recharge and refocus their attention.

Brain breaks can take various forms, including stretching exercises, deep breathing exercises, quick energizing games, or even short mindfulness activities. By incorporating these play tactics into the daily routine, educators can create a positive and energized learning environment that supports student well-being for the whole class.

Numerous studies have examined the relationship between play and academic performance. The findings consistently demonstrate the positive impact on student learning and education.

A study conducted by the American Academy of Pediatrics found that children who had more recess time performed better academically and exhibited improved social skills compared to those with less recess. The researchers concluded that recess provides crucial opportunities for children to develop cognitive, emotional, and social skills necessary for academic success (Barros, Silver, & Stein, 2009).

Furthermore, a meta-analysis published in the *Journal of School Health* found a significant positive relationship between physical activity and academic performance. The study concluded that regular physical activity can enhance cognitive function, attentiveness, and academic achievement.

These research findings support the importance of providing students with regular opportunities for breaks to optimize learning.

Strategies for Incorporating Recess, Play, and Brain Breaks in the Classroom

Incorporating recess, play, and brain breaks into the school day is crucial for promoting student well-being and enhancing the educational experience. These activities play a pivotal role in fostering a holistic approach to education and can significantly contribute to students' social, emotional, and cognitive development. By implementing various strategies, schools and teachers can ensure these become integral components of the curriculum, ultimately creating a more engaging and supportive learning environment.

Allocating specific time slots for unstructured play and physical activity is imperative. For example, teachers can organize outdoor games such as tag, soccer, or relay races to promote exercise and social interaction among students.

Integrating play into the curriculum through play-based learning activities offers students hands-on, interactive experiences that make learning more engaging and enjoyable. For instance, in a science lesson about ecosystems, students can participate in a simulation where they act out different roles of animals and plants within an ecosystem, promoting critical thinking and understanding of complex concepts.

Some activities can be designed to be done beside the desk, such as quick stretching exercises, deep breathing techniques, or guided mindfulness activities. Games like GoNoodle, which offers interactive exercises, can be incorporated to make class more engaging and enjoyable for students. For example, a quick GoNoodle dance or yoga session can help students release tension and boost their energy levels.

What teachers have available in the classroom matters as well. Having age-appropriate toys, games, and sensory tools in the classroom supports active play and creativity, fostering inclusivity and stimulating students' development. For instance, providing building blocks or puzzles can encourage problem-solving skills, while sensory tools like stress balls or fidget toys can help students regulate their emotions and stay engaged in their lessons.

In addition to scheduled recess and brain breaks, integrating movement into daily classroom activities further enhances student engagement and learning. Incorporating movement breaks between lessons, using standing desks or flexible seating options, and organizing active learning games can keep students physically active while class goes on. For example, teachers can incorporate short physical activities like jumping jacks or stretching exercises between lessons to energize students and improve their focus.

By implementing these strategies and providing specific examples, educators can create a balanced approach that promotes student well-being, positive behavior, and academic success. As you can see, it's crucial for schools to recognize the significance of a holistic approach to education.

The Role of Teachers in Facilitating Recess, Play, and Brain Breaks

As you navigate your role as an educator, you hold a pivotal position in nurturing a comprehensive learning environment that prioritizes physical activity, unstructured play, and mental rejuvenation. These elements play a crucial role in shaping your students' overall well-being and success in your classroom. Your proactive approach to integrate these elements into your teaching practices strengthens your impact on student development.

During break times, you can encourage physical activity and unstructured play by creating an environment conducive to exploration. Your students can benefit greatly from active play experiences, such as participating in games or using diverse play equipment like balls, jump ropes, and building blocks, all of which foster physical release and social interaction. Your encouragement and facilitation of these activities not only promote physical health but also enhance students' social skills and emotional well-being.

Incorporating play-based learning activities into your daily lessons is another effective approach to engaging students and deepening their understanding of academic concepts. Designing interactive games, hands-on experiments, and collaborative projects that promote problem-solving and critical thinking skills can make learning enjoyable and meaningful for your students. Your creativity in designing these activities will allow your students to actively participate in their learning process, leading to a deeper level of comprehension and retention of knowledge.

Brain breaks are valuable moments during the day when you can help your students recharge mentally and refocus their attention. These breaks may include brief physical exercises, interactive puzzles, or guided relaxation techniques, all of which can contribute to your students' cognitive well-being and stress reduction. Your guidance during these breaks can help your class develop mindfulness and self-regulation skills, preparing them to manage academic challenges with resilience and focus.

In addition to facilitating these activities, you can provide guidance and support to ensure inclusive play and effective participation in learning experiences. By promoting teamwork, cooperation, and offering encouragement, you can create an environment where all your students can thrive academically, socially, and emotionally. Your dedication to fostering a positive and inclusive classroom culture can foster a sense of belonging and motivation among your students, setting the stage for their long-term success.

Your commitment to fostering a holistic educational experience is essential for your students' overall development and long-term academic success. Your efforts contribute significantly to creating a positive and supportive learning environment that values physical health, social interactions, mental well-being, and academic growth. Through your proactive approach and dedication to student well-being, you empower students to reach their full potential and become lifelong learners.

Overcoming Challenges in Implementing These Strategies

One common challenge is the perception that there isn't enough time in the school day to allocate for recess, play, and brain breaks. In some high-performing countries like Finland, students receive fifteen minutes of recess for every forty-five minutes of instruction, amounting to fifteen minutes of recess every hour. This approach acknowledges that these breaks not only refresh students but also positively impact their learning. Research has shown that these activities can improve student focus and productivity, leading to more efficient use of instructional time.

A great example of this is Tim Walker. He was an American teacher who traveled to Finland to teach 5th grade. He has recounted several times how he tried to extend learning time in his classes to cover more content rather than taking a break every fifteen minutes. He said his students would quickly become disengaged and were almost zombie like after ninety minutes. Then he decided to embrace the fifteen minute break, and after teaching for forty-five minutes, his students would get the fifteen minutes just like the other classes. He said the transformation was immediate. After the fifteen minute breaks, his students would come into the classroom with a bounce in their steps and be ready to focus on their work.

Additionally, Finland's education system emphasizes project-based learning activities over the traditional "sit and get" style. This approach fosters creativity, critical thinking, and collaboration among students, contributing to a more comprehensive learning experience.

Moreover, Finland's approach to standardized testing differs significantly from many other countries. Students in Finland do not take standardized tests until high school, allowing for a focus on holistic learning rather than test preparation. Despite this, Finland consistently outperforms many other nations on international assessments like the Programme for International Student Assessment (PISA), demonstrating the effectiveness of their education system in producing high-achieving students. (Johnson, 2019)

By incorporating elements such as ample recess time, project-based learning, limited standardized testing, and a focus on comprehensive learning, schools can emulate successful strategies seen in countries like Finland. It has enhanced student well-being and academic performance time and time again.

In addition to time constraints, another challenge schools may face is the lack of resources, such as play equipment or teacher training. Addressing this challenge involves exploring avenues for acquiring necessary resources, such as seeking community partnerships or grants. Additionally, providing professional development opportunities for teachers can enhance their ability to incorporate play and brain breaks into their lessons effectively. By leveraging community support and pursuing external funding sources, schools can overcome resource limitations and ensure that students have access to the tools and opportunities needed to benefit from these activities.

Apart from time constraints and resource limitations, schools may also encounter challenges related to administrative support and policy alignment. Administrative support is essential for implementing these initiatives effectively. That includes allocating budgetary resources, providing professional development opportunities, and establishing policies that prioritize student well-being and holistic development.

Policy alignment is another critical aspect that schools need to consider. Ensuring that school policies and practices align with the goals of incorporating recess, play, and brain breaks can be challenging, especially if there are conflicting priorities or outdated policies that hinder the implementation of these strategies. Schools may need to review and revise existing policies to create a conducive environment for integrating these activities into the daily schedule.

Furthermore, teacher confidence and expertise in implementation can also pose a challenge. Not all teachers may initially feel confident integrating these activities into their teaching practices. To address this, schools can offer support and training to build teachers' confidence and expertise gradually. Professional development workshops and ongoing support from school leadership can empower teachers to incorporate these activities into their teaching in a way that enhances student well-being and learning experiences.

By recognizing and addressing challenges related to time constraints, resource limitations, and teacher confidence, schools can successfully implement recess, play, and brain breaks to create a more supportive learning environment. Overcoming these challenges is crucial for student well-being and academic success.

The Benefits of Movement in Learning

In the wise words of neuroscientist Panksepp, "We have to know how to use play properly and make sure our children get plenty of it" (Panksepp, 2011). Research has consistently shown that incorporating movement and brain breaks positively impact student behavior, focus, attention, and academic performance. Movement activities play a crucial role in helping students self-regulate their emotions, stay focused on tasks, and burn off excess energy. By recognizing the importance of these strategies, educators can create a balanced approach that cultivates well-rounded individuals.

Scheduling regular movement breaks and incorporating brain breaks are crucial to create a positive learning environment. These practices not only foster positive behavior but also boost academic achievement, setting students up for long-term success. It is time to embrace the power of movement and brain breaks and transform the classroom experience for the better.

These strategies offer crucial outlets for physical activity, social development, and mental refreshment. They positively impact behavior, focus, and overall academic performance.

It is essential to acknowledge that these practices should never be compromised. As an educator, you have the power to make this happen! Instead of taking away movement breaks, you could explore natural consequences for addressing your students' issues. For instance, if a student struggles with focus, integrating short brain breaks during class can provide a constructive outlet for their energy, aiding you in maintaining their attentiveness without sacrificing precious learning time. Alternatively, addressing disruptive behavior through collaborative problem-solving reinforces positive social skills, ensuring a balanced and effective approach to the way you manage your classroom.

As a teacher, your commitment to nurturing a positive learning environment involves valuing and implementing these strategies. By recognizing the impact of movement and brain breaks, you have the power to enhance academic achievement and foster holistic development.

Remember how I allowed a student who was struggling with focus to do push-ups as a consequence for disruptive behavior? Surprisingly, his behavior improved significantly in my class compared to others where traditional disciplinary measures were employed. You can find the same success!

By incorporating such creative and effective approaches, you will not only enhance academic achievement but also foster holistic development. When you embrace these practices, it will demonstrate your dedication to the comprehensive well-being and success of your students. Your class will notice, and much like I experienced with my struggling student, it will be worth it.

9

Conflict Resolution and Mediation

Joan of Arc, a young peasant girl from Domrémy, France, felt a calling to support Charles VII and liberate France from English control during the Hundred Years' War. Despite facing skepticism and disbelief, Joan's unwavering faith and conviction led her to seek an audience with Charles VII.

Against all odds, Joan convinced the French king to grant her authority to lead his troops. Her lack of formal military training was overshadowed by her courage, determination, and unyielding belief in the righteousness of their cause. She became a symbol of hope and unity among the French forces.

Joan's strategic insights and fearless leadership were instrumental in key battles, notably the siege of Orléans in 1429. The city, surrounded by English forces, seemed on the brink of defeat until Joan's daring assault lifted the siege, marking a turning point in the war.

Despite facing criticism, opposition within the French court, and accusations of heresy from her enemies, Joan remained steadfast in her mission. Her conflict with the English forces and internal skepticism within France only strengthened her resolve.

Joan of Arc's legacy has extended far beyond her military successes. Her ability to unite disparate factions and inspire others serves as a timeless example of effective leadership during conflict. She navigated challenges with grace and determination, showing that resilience in the face of adversity can lead to a profound impact and lasting change.

Regardless of age or background, Joan's story teaches us that embracing conflict with courage and conviction can be transformative. The lesson is not about avoiding conflict but about facing it head-on, using it as a catalyst for growth and positive outcomes. When handled with integrity and a sense of purpose, conflict can ignite innovation, foster collaboration, and ultimately pave the way for meaningful progress and success.

For educators, embracing conflict means recognizing the diversity of perspectives among students and colleagues. It involves creating a supportive and inclusive environment where differing viewpoints are valued and conflicts are seen as opportunities for learning and improvement.

Similarly, students can learn valuable life skills by engaging in healthy debates, addressing conflicts respectfully, and working together to find common ground. These experiences not only enhance critical thinking and communication skills but also promote understanding and cooperation.

In essence, Joan of Arc's legacy reminds us that conflict, when met with courage and integrity, can be a catalyst for positive change and meaningful growth, both on the battlefield and in the realm of education. It's about transforming challenges into opportunities and harnessing the power of conflict to foster a culture of learning.

Understanding Conflict in Educational Settings

Conflict is an intrinsic aspect of human interactions, encompassing any disagreement that arises from differing perspectives or needs. In educational settings, conflicts may arise from various sources, such as academic challenges, interpersonal relationships, or classroom dynamics.

For example, students may disagree on group project roles or experience conflicts due to misunderstandings or cultural differences. If left unaddressed, these tensions can impact students' academic performance, well-being, and the overall classroom atmosphere.

One common misconception about conflict is that it is always disruptive and damaging. While conflicts can indeed lead to tension and emotional distress, they also offer valuable insights into students' perspectives and needs. By addressing conflicts proactively and constructively, educators create a safe and supportive space for students to express themselves, resolve differences, and develop essential social-emotional skills.

Moreover, conflicts provide opportunities for students to learn valuable lessons in communication and problem-solving. When students engage in constructive dialogue to resolve conflicts, they practice active listening, empathy, and negotiation skills, which are essential for navigating real-world challenges and healthy relationships. Through the process of conflict resolution, students learn to consider alternative perspectives and work towards mutually beneficial solutions.

Let's say, for instance, that two students working on a group project have different ideas about how to approach a problem. Initially, this may lead to disagreement and tension. However, through open communication and collaboration, they can combine their ideas to create an innovative solution. Not only will the problem be solved, but both students will have grown and strengthened their teamwork skills.

Additionally, conflicts arising from cultural differences among students can become positive learning experiences. Educators can facilitate discussions where students share their perspectives, learn from each other's experiences, and develop greater empathy and cultural awareness, leading to a more inclusive and harmonious classroom environment.

It's important for educators to recognize that conflicts in educational settings are not inherently negative but rather natural occurrences that can contribute to students' social and emotional growth. When conflicts are managed effectively, they can foster a positive classroom climate, promote a sense of community and belonging, and enhance the overall learning experience. Conflict resolution skills are crucial for students' social and emotional development, equipping them with the tools to navigate conflicts respectfully, collaboratively, and empathetically.

Now it's time to examine strategies that can help educators address conflicts effectively, promote positive relationships, and enrich their students' learning experiences. These strategies will provide practical tools and approaches tailored to the classroom environment. By empowering educators with the knowledge and skills to navigate conflicts constructively, we can create inclusive and supportive learning environments where every student can thrive.

Embracing Conflict: Unveiling Its Positive Power and Growth Opportunities

Positive aspects of conflict are often overlooked due to its traditional perception as a negative and disruptive force. One of the reasons conflict is often viewed as negative, especially in educational settings, is because many teachers tend to naturally value agreeableness, as mentioned earlier. This personality trait is characterized by a strong desire for harmony, a tendency to avoid confrontation, and a reluctance to hurt anyone's feelings. As a result, teachers may hesitate to engage in conflicts or address issues directly, fearing that it might disrupt the classroom atmosphere or damage relationships. This inclination towards maintaining peace and avoiding discord can contribute to the perception that conflict is inherently negative and should be avoided whenever possible.

Firstly, reframing perception involves recognizing conflict as an opportunity for personal and collective development. Rather than viewing conflict solely as a source of tension and discomfort, we can see it as a catalyst for growth and learning. Remember how Joan of Arc wasn't afraid to embrace conflict? Conflict arises from differing perspectives, interests, and needs, highlighting the diversity and complexity within individuals and groups. Embracing this diversity can lead to richer discussions, deeper insights, and enhanced understanding among stakeholders.

Moreover, when handled constructively, conflict has the potential to yield positive outcomes. Instead of avoiding or suppressing conflicts, engaging with them openly and respectfully can foster empathy, communication skills, and conflict resolution strategies. Constructive conflict management involves active listening, seeking common ground, and finding mutually beneficial solutions. This approach not only resolves immediate issues but also strengthens relationships, builds trust, and promotes a culture of collaboration and innovation.

One of the key benefits of conflict is its ability to stimulate creativity and problem-solving skills. When individuals or groups encounter challenges or disagreements, they are prompted to think critically and consider alternative solutions. This process of divergent thinking can lead to innovative approaches and breakthroughs in addressing complex problems. In educational settings, encouraging constructive debate and dialogue can inspire students to think creatively, question assumptions, and develop problem-solving abilities.

Furthermore, conflict promotes the exploration of alternative viewpoints and perspectives. Rather than adhering to a single perspective or approach, engaging with conflicting viewpoints allows individuals to consider different angles, challenge assumptions, and broaden their understanding of complex issues. This diversity of perspectives fosters a more comprehensive and nuanced understanding of topics, leading to informed decision-making and well-rounded solutions.

Additionally, conflict encourages collaboration and teamwork by bringing individuals together to address shared challenges or goals. When managed effectively, conflicts can serve as opportunities to build trust, enhance communication, and strengthen relationships. Collaborative conflict resolution involves fostering a sense of mutual respect and working towards common objectives. This collaborative mindset not only improves group dynamics but also promotes a culture of cooperation and shared success.

Another benefit of conflict is its role in fostering resilience and adaptability. Dealing with conflicts requires individuals to navigate uncertainty, manage emotions, and persevere through challenges. Overcoming conflicts builds resilience by helping those involved develop coping mechanisms, emotional intelligence, and problem-solving skills. This resilience prepares individuals to face future challenges with confidence, flexibility, and a positive mindset.

In conclusion, conflict has several positive aspects that are often overshadowed by its negative perception. By reframing our understanding of conflict and recognizing its potential, we can harness its benefits to promote collaboration and foster resilience. Embracing constructive conflict management strategies empowers individuals and groups to navigate challenges, build stronger relationships, and achieve shared goals.

Strategies for Positive Classroom Dynamics

Navigating conflict in the classroom requires a proactive, positive approach that fosters a deeper understanding of conflict resolution among students. It's important for teachers to discuss conflict openly and demonstrate how it can be handled constructively, emphasizing that conflict is a natural part of life and can lead to growth and positive outcomes when managed effectively.

One crucial strategy is to initiate discussions about conflict and its role in personal and interpersonal development. Teachers can create opportunities for students to share their experiences with conflict, discuss common challenges they face, and explore different perspectives on resolving conflicts. By framing conflict as a normal and manageable aspect of life, teachers can help students develop a healthy attitude towards conflict resolution and build their confidence in addressing conflicts when they arise.

Moreover, it's essential to be proactive rather than reactive when dealing with conflicts among students. Reacting impulsively to conflicts often leads to negative outcomes and can escalate tensions.

For example, instead of taking away recess for all students just because one or two students couldn't behave, teachers can use individualized interventions, such as having private conversations with disruptive students or implementing targeted behavior plans, to address the root causes of conflict more effectively.

Another essential strategy is to focus on building relationships and fostering a sense of community in the classroom. Teachers can incorporate activities that promote teamwork and communication skills, thereby helping students develop positive relationships and constructively navigate conflicts. For instance, organizing team-building activities where students work together towards a common goal promotes collaboration and teamwork. Implementing peer support systems where students can mentor each other, provide emotional support, and build a sense of belonging within the classroom community also contributes to a positive classroom environment.

It's also vital to focus on the issue, not on the individual, when addressing conflicts in the classroom. Conflicts may arise from misunderstandings, differing perspectives, or unmet needs rather than personal attacks. It's crucial for teachers to differentiate between behavior and personality. Likewise, they need to address specific behaviors causing conflict while supporting students in understanding and managing their emotions. During conflict resolution discussions, emphasizing understanding the underlying reasons behind conflicts, such as differences in opinions, values, or experiences, rather than attributing blame to individuals, fosters a more respectful and constructive dialogue. Using "I" statements and teaching active listening skills, such as paraphrasing and summarizing, also helps students express their feelings and concerns without attacking or accusing others, promoting a deeper understanding of each other's perspectives.

Furthermore, focusing on the future, not on the conflict, is essential for effective conflict resolution. Teachers can emphasize the importance of learning from conflicts, understanding different viewpoints, and using them as opportunities to strengthen collaboration and problem-solving skills. Encouraging students to reflect on conflicts, identify ways to prevent similar situations in the future, and work towards common goals promotes a positive and growth-oriented mindset. Teachers can reinforce a continuous growth mindset by facilitating a reflective discussion where students analyze what they've learned from conflicts and brainstorm strategies to prevent further issues. Additionally, incorporating role-playing scenarios or case studies that depict common conflicts in school settings allows students to practice problem-solving and decision-making skills in a simulated environment, further enhancing their ability to navigate conflicts constructively.

By implementing these strategies, teachers create a positive and supportive classroom environment that promotes healthy relationships, constructive conflict resolution, and personal growth among students. These efforts not only help students develop essential social and emotional skills but also contribute to a more harmonious and productive learning environment.

The Transformative Benefits of Handling Conflict in the Classroom

Handling conflict in the classroom yields numerous benefits that contribute significantly to students' social, emotional, and cognitive development. One of the key advantages is the promotion of emotional intelligence and social skills among students. Engaging in conflict resolution helps students identify and manage their emotions effectively. It also fosters empathy and enhances communication skills, which are crucial for building positive relationships and succeeding in various social contexts.

Additionally, addressing conflicts in the classroom fosters critical thinking and problem-solving abilities. It allows students to learn to think critically, analyze situations, and devise creative solutions to conflicts. This cultivates cognitive skills that are transferable to academic tasks, real-life challenges, and future professional endeavors. When it's handled the right way, this turns conflict management into a valuable learning experience.

Conflict resolution also plays a pivotal role in enhancing communication skills among students. Through constructive dialogue during conflict resolution, students practice expressing their thoughts, feelings, and needs clearly and assertively. They also develop active listening skills and learn to understand and acknowledge others' perspectives, contributing to effective interpersonal communication.

Moreover, handling conflicts in the classroom builds resilience and emotional regulation among students. Dealing with adversity and learning to manage stress and regulate emotions effectively are essential aspects of conflict resolution. Students develop resilience by overcoming obstacles, learning from experiences, and adapting to changing situations, which are valuable life skills that contribute to their overall well-being and success.

Furthermore, conflict resolution encourages collaboration and teamwork among students. Addressing conflicts involves cooperation, compromise, and collective problem-solving, fostering a culture of collaboration and teamwork in the classroom. These collaborative skills are crucial for success in group projects, team activities, and collaborative learning environments, preparing students for future collaborative endeavors.

Additionally, engaging in conflict resolution promotes respect and empathy. This is when students learn to appreciate diverse perspectives, listen empathetically, and respond respectfully to others' feelings and needs. This cultivation of respect and empathy creates a supportive, inclusive classroom environment where students feel valued, respected, and heard.

Moreover, conflict resolution teaches students various conflict management strategies such as active listening, assertive communication, problem-solving, negotiation, and compromise. These strategies empower students to address conflicts constructively, resolve differences peacefully, and build stronger relationships, contributing to a positive and harmonious classroom atmosphere.

Handling conflict in the classroom promotes growth and

learning for students. It also encourages self-reflection, self-awareness, and personal growth as students navigate challenges and learn from experiences. Conflict resolution fosters a growth mindset—the belief that abilities can be developed through effort and perseverance. Students who view conflicts as opportunities for learning and growth embrace challenges, seek feedback, and strive for continuous improvement, leading to overall academic and personal growth.

Finally, navigating conflicts in the classroom requires more than just strategies and techniques; it calls for a deep understanding of human emotions, empathy, and resilience from teachers like you. Just as Joan of Arc displayed unwavering resolve and courage in the face of adversity, you can approach conflicts with a similar mindset, recognizing that you are dealing with children who are learning to navigate their emotions and interactions.

Empathy plays a crucial role in conflict resolution, as it can allow you to see conflicts from your students' perspectives and understand the underlying emotions driving their behaviors. By empathizing with students, you can cultivate a supportive and understanding environment where conflicts are seen as opportunities for growth and learning rather than disruptions.

Patience is another key attribute that can help you navigate conflicts. It's important to remember that children are still developing their emotional regulation skills and may not always express themselves effectively. Patience can allow you to give your students the time and space they need to process their emotions and communicate their needs during conflicts.

Understanding is also vital in conflict resolution. If you seek to understand the root causes of conflicts, it will be worth it. By understanding the underlying reasons behind conflicts, teachers can address them more effectively and help students develop problem-solving skills and emotional resilience.

Incorporating these qualities of empathy, patience, and understanding into conflict resolution strategies creates a holistic approach that fosters positive relationships, promotes emotional intelligence, and enhances students' social and emotional well-being. Just as Joan of Arc's resilience and unwavering resolve inspired her followers, you can approach conflicts with empathy, patience, and understanding. The end result, of course, is inspiring your students to learn from conflicts, grow from challenges, and develop into compassionate, resilient individuals.

10

Empowering Students for Lasting Change

If you're like many teachers, chances are some of the ideas presented in this book might have been unfamiliar to you. Having had the privilege of traveling extensively, I've engaged with educators worldwide, and concepts such as the Pygmalion Effect, Educere, and divergent learning often emerge as novel to teachers around the country.

However, at their core, they revolve around the idea of empowering students to assume control of their learning journey, while also emphasizing the crucial role teachers play in establishing connections needed to facilitate it. This chapter serves to empower you as an educator to actively become a catalyst for change.

Where traditional methods are under scrutiny and student needs are evolving, the need for transformation is more urgent. This shift isn't a theoretical exercise; it's an invitation for educators everywhere to embrace a new approach that moves beyond conventional teaching methods.

Student-centered learning is our practical guide in this journey, putting students at the forefront of the education landscape. This is a move away from the old model where students passively receive information to where they actively participate in the learning process.

At its core, this transformative approach is about recognizing that lasting change involves empowering students both academically and emotionally. At the heart of it all lies the crucial element of relationships. That's because education, fundamentally, is all about relationships. It's about the connection between educators and students, fostering an environment of trust, understanding, and mutual respect.

This call to action goes beyond theory. It demands a practical shift in the educator's role—from being the sole provider of knowledge to being a facilitator and guide in the student's learning journey. It requires educators to let go of traditional hierarchies and empower students to actively participate in shaping their educational experiences.

When educators establish connections with their students, it opens avenues for collaboration and engagement, as well as a shared commitment to the learning process. In such an environment, students feel not only supported but also motivated to take an active role in their education.

This commitment to uncovering the unique passions and strengths within each student recognizes that every child brings distinct talents and interests to the learning environment. Educators must not just identify these strengths but actively nurture them, and then guide students toward finding their voice and becoming their best selves.

The practical aspect of implementing student-centered learning is about moving beyond traditional boundaries and embracing the needs of students. This is when educators become architects of change, fostering an environment that imparts knowledge while instilling purpose and resilience in every student.

This commitment to practical change is an acknowledgment that the empowerment of our students is a tangible path—one that requires our immediate attention and action. As we embark on this journey, let us embrace this shift and become agents of transformative change for our students, recognizing that at the core of this transformation is strong relationships.

Cultivating a Growth Mindset

The concept of a growth mindset is not just a theoretical construct; it is a mandate for immediate action. It urges educators not only to comprehend it but to actively instill it in the hearts and minds of students. This call is more than a mere challenge to embrace difficulties; it is an urgent plea to seek difficulties as opportunities for growth. Naturally, it turns into practical strategies, guiding educators on how to consistently praise the process of learning itself.

Furthermore, fostering a growth mindset involves creating an environment where mistakes are viewed not as failures but as stepping stones towards mastery. Emphasizing the importance of a positive attitude towards challenges, educators can encourage students to approach obstacles with curiosity and a belief in their ability to overcome them. Integrating reflective practices into the curriculum allows students to analyze their own learning processes, reinforcing the idea that progress is a continuous journey.

As mentioned earlier, success, when aligned with students' unique strengths, plays a crucial role in nurturing a growth mindset. When students experience success, they often become more confident and willing to venture into new or more challenging tasks. Recognizing individual achievements builds a foundation for students to perceive challenges not as threats but as opportunities to further develop their capabilities.

In addition, collaborative learning experiences can play a pivotal role in cultivating a growth mindset. By fostering a sense of community within the classroom, educators can create spaces where students feel comfortable sharing ideas and learning from one another. Group projects and interactive discussions provide opportunities for students to appreciate diverse perspectives and understand that learning is not a solitary endeavor but a collective effort.

This holistic approach extends beyond the classroom, involving parents and caregivers in the process of nurturing a growth mindset. Open communication channels with families enable educators to reinforce the importance of resilience and a positive approach to challenges both at school and in the broader context of life.

In essence, cultivating a growth mindset is not just about academic success; it is about equipping students with the mindset and skills necessary to navigate the complexities of an ever-changing world. It involves creating an ecosystem where the journey of learning is celebrated and embraced, preparing students to face challenges with confidence and a belief in their innate capacity for growth.

Student-Centered Learning

In the pursuit of educational excellence, the call to action transcends traditional teaching methods. It stands as a resolute directive for transformative change, urging educators to liberate classrooms from the shackles of convention. This imperative beckons the metamorphosis of learning spaces into dynamic environments, where students cease to be passive recipients and instead emerge as active architects of their educational journey.

Student-centered learning is not a mere suggestion; it is a clarion call for educators to redefine their roles and embrace a paradigm shift in the educational landscape. The narrative unfolds as a guidebook, navigating practical ways for teachers to weave student empowerment into the very fabric of their classrooms.

At the heart of this transformative approach lies the recognition that every child brings a unique tapestry of passions and strengths to the learning table. It challenges educators not only to acknowledge this individuality but to actively engage in the process of unveiling and nurturing it. This is not a peripheral aspect of teaching; it is a fundamental responsibility. Teachers are called upon not just to disseminate knowledge but to be mentors in the truest sense—guides who aid students in discovering their voices and empowering them to be the very best versions of themselves.

Central to the student-centered philosophy is the belief that each child possesses an intrinsic purpose waiting to be uncovered. It is a purpose that goes beyond academic achievements, because it is intertwined with their strengths and personal aspirations. As educators, our mandate is to facilitate this journey of self-discovery. We are entrusted with the task of creating an environment where students feel empowered to explore and articulate their aspirations. This mission extends far beyond textbooks and standardized curricula, because the goal is to cultivate individuals who are not only academically adept but also self-aware and ready to contribute meaningfully to the world.

Practical implementation of student-centered learning requires a departure from traditional top-down teaching methods. Educators must relinquish the reins of absolute authority and, instead, become collaborators in the learning process. At last, students are not just consumers of information but active contributors to the shaping of their educational experiences. They are involved in decision-making processes, given agency in goal setting, and invited to actively engage in the co-creation of knowledge.

For example, empowering students to take the lead in organizing extracurricular activities, clubs, or projects that align with their interests and passions fosters leadership skills. It also naturally teaches them how to collaborate with peers, and how to contribute positively to their school community.

Allowing students to participate in setting learning goals and objectives for themselves also plays a crucial role in student agency. This practice fosters a sense of ownership and responsibility in their education, enabling students to identify areas for growth and take proactive steps in their learning journey. Similarly, giving students autonomy in project-based learning by allowing them to choose topics, conduct research, and present their findings promotes critical thinking and problem-solving skills. This approach ensures that students actively engage in hands-on learning experiences that are meaningful and relevant to their interests and learning needs.

Furthermore, when teachers co-create classroom rules and norms with students it promotes a positive, inclusive learning environment. By collaborating with students to establish classroom rules and norms, teachers allow students a sense of ownership and accountability, fostering a community of mutual respect among peers. When teachers empower students to take charge of their learning, they can help create a learning environment that values their voices and contributions.

Of course, the metamorphosis to student-centered learning is not without its challenges. It requires educators to be flexible and willing to embrace a more facilitative role. However, the rewards are profound—a classroom where learning is not a one-size-fits-all model but a tailored experience that resonates with each student's individuality. When educators recognize and celebrate the uniqueness within each student, it nurtures an environment where passions are kindled, strengths are honed, and purposes are uncovered. This is when students find their voice and their very best selves. It is a journey toward transformative change—one classroom at a time.

Encouraging Critical Thinking

The departure from rote memorization is crucial if we are to prioritize critical thinking in our classrooms. We need a paradigm shift, classrooms where we prepare students for life, not just exams. It's essential to foster critical thinking and encourage students to question assumptions and engage in independent analysis. By doing so, educators can empower a generation of innovators and problem solvers who can navigate the complexities of the world.

Critical thinking is a tool for students to uncover their purpose and contribute meaningfully to society. While the focus on critical thinking is paramount, it's important to note that memorization still holds its place in the learning process. However, it should not be the primary focus. Instead, it should complement critical thinking by providing a foundation of knowledge that students can analyze, evaluate, and apply in various contexts. This balanced approach equips students with the essential skills to thrive in a rapidly changing world while also acknowledging the value of foundational knowledge.

To initiate this transformative journey, educators like you must go beyond traditional teaching methods and embrace practices that stimulate intellectual curiosity. Fostering an environment that encourages questioning assumptions and independent analysis is crucial.

For example, you could incorporate real-world problem-solving scenarios into the curriculum, such as creating a project that requires students to identify and propose solutions to a community issue. Projects like this can provide your students with practical applications for critical thinking skills. You can encourage open-ended discussions, where students explore various perspectives and defend their viewpoints. This can also contribute to the development of critical thinking and problem-solving abilities. Additionally, the integration of interdisciplinary approaches can broaden students' cognitive horizons, encouraging them to connect knowledge across different domains and think holistically. By striking a balance between foundational knowledge and critical thinking skills, you can best prepare your students for the challenges and opportunities of the future.

Fostering Creativity and Innovation

Creativity is not simply a skill to be taught; it's a demand that must be met. There is an intense need for educators to transform their classrooms into vibrant hubs of creativity. We must find practical ways to encourage students to think beyond conventional boundaries, challenge the status quo, and view challenges as opportunities for innovation. Teachers must find ways to draw out creativity from their students, highlighting the potential for every student to be a game-changer. The truth is that within every child lies unique passions and potential innovations waiting to be unearthed, ultimately contributing to their broader sense of purpose.

To foster creativity, educators should create an atmosphere that values curiosity and risk-taking. Encouraging students to pursue projects that align with their interests and passions can unleash their creative potential. Integrating arts and project-based learning into the curriculum can provide avenues for students to express their creativity. Additionally, educators should celebrate diverse forms of intelligence, acknowledging that creativity manifests in various ways. By providing constructive feedback and creating a supportive environment, teachers like you can nurture a culture where creativity is not just encouraged but celebrated.

I've seen this play out in my own life more times that I can count. I recall a high school math teacher I knew who exemplified innovation and creativity in his teaching methods. He would have students divide into groups and give them a budget to plan out vacations. The task was to create a detailed itinerary within the given budget. What made this exercise truly innovative was that the teacher would choose the best vacation plan created by the students and take that vacation each summer. This not only showcased the teacher's creativity in engaging students but also provided a real-world, relevant application for the students' creative thinking and budgeting skills. Magnificently, it also proved the trust and value that the teacher had placed in his students. They were in a connected relationship where he put stake in what they thought, and the students rewarded his trust in them year after year. It was a brilliant example of how educators can infuse creativity and innovation into the learning process, creating a dynamic and engaging environment for students to thrive.

Developing Leadership Skills

Leadership is not a distant goal but a skill to be cultivated from the beginning. It's important for educators to recognize and nurture leadership potential in students. It involves providing opportunities for students to lead, make decisions, and inspire others. When leadership becomes an expectation, it is not confined to a select few but can be revealed in each student. It underscores that part of our job as educators is to empower students to lead with purpose, leveraging our students' strengths and passions for impactful leadership.

To develop leadership skills, educators should create opportunities for students to take on leadership roles within the classroom and school community. Assigning responsibilities that require decision-making, collaboration, and communication can contribute to leadership development. Providing mentorship and guidance can help students identify their leadership styles and strengths. Additionally, incorporating leadership development programs and extracurricular activities can further enhance students' abilities to lead with purpose.

An inspiring example of fostering leadership skills recently took place in a high school near me. Their student-led initiative was truly mind-blowing. The school established a student council where members were responsible for organizing school events, representing student interests, and initiating community service projects. The faculty provided guidance and support, allowing the students to take ownership of their roles and make meaningful contributions to the school environment. This initiative not only empowered students to lead with purpose but also created a sense of ownership and responsibility among the student body. By providing such platforms for student leadership, any educator can instill valuable leadership skills and cultivate a sense of agency and initiative in their students. Strategies like this can prepare them to become effective future leaders.

By integrating these approaches into the educational framework, you can play a pivotal role in nurturing leadership potential and developing critical thinking skills in your students. You have the power to equip them with the abilities necessary to thrive in our rapidly evolving world.

Digital Literacy and Technological Empowerment

The remarkable evolution of technology within the span of a single lifetime, from the era of electric typewriters to the current landscape of advanced computers, showcases the rapid strides made in the digital age. This transformative journey underscores an opportunity for both educators and students alike to engage with the dynamic nature of technological progress.

In a few short decades, the digital landscape has witnessed the emergence of revolutionary tools and platforms. The advent of Google, for example, has fundamentally reshaped how information is accessed and processed, placing a vast reservoir of knowledge at our fingertips. Concurrently, social media has become another transformative force, redefining communication and collaboration while offering novel avenues for expression and connection. These technological developments, now seamlessly woven into our daily lives, serve as powerful instruments capable of propelling students into a future marked by unforeseen advancements.

As we peer into the future, it's crucial to acknowledge that the technological journey is far from over. The trajectory of innovation continues its upward climb, presenting students with opportunities and challenges that we cannot even conceive of today. Standing on the brink of unknown technological frontiers, we assume a pivotal role in preparing students not only for the current state of technology but for the ever-evolving landscape that lies ahead.

Even the integration of artificial intelligence (AI) into various aspects of our lives has become increasingly prevalent. AI technologies, ranging from virtual assistants to advanced machine learning algorithms, are reshaping industries and influencing how we interact with information and the world around us. Educators like you can prepare students for a future where AI will play a significant role in various fields. You can emphasize the importance of understanding and collaborating with these technologies which will help prepare your students for an exciting future.

Navigating this landscape demands that students possess not only technical skills but also a mindset characterized by adaptability and a commitment to continuous learning. The tools and platforms driving careers and shaping futures are poised to evolve in ways that are beyond our imagination.

By acknowledging the transformative power of technology and its potential for future developments, you can inspire your students to become agile navigators of the digital world. You can prepare them for existing technologies as well as the capacity to embrace the innovations of tomorrow. In doing so, your students can prepare to be architects of the technological landscape yet to unfold.

Everything Comes Full Circle: People and Relationships

Prioritizing the emotional well-being of students is a comprehensive and holistic directive. It is not just about teaching subjects but equipping students for life. It's essential for educators to cultivate self-awareness, empathy, and resilience in their students. The classroom needs tools for conflict resolution, stress management, and emotional regulation. This is where we can prepare students for the inevitable challenges they will face in life, ensuring they are emotionally resilient and equipped for success beyond the classroom. A large part of our role as educators is to nurture their emotional intelligence, helping them navigate challenges with purpose and resilience.

Likewise, it's vital to cultivate people-centric environments in our classrooms. Amidst the focus on technological advancement and academic preparedness, we must recognize that everything comes back to people and relationships. While embracing the advancements in technology and academic curriculum, we must also prioritize the nurturing of interpersonal skills and relationship building. The emphasis on Social and Emotional Learning (SEL) serves as a poignant reminder that at the core of education lies the development of compassionate and resilient individuals who can navigate the complexities of human interaction and collaboration.

You can prioritize social and emotional learning in your

classroom by integrating SEL practices into your curriculum, thereby creating a supportive and emotionally intelligent learning environment. By incorporating mindfulness activities, fostering open communication, and providing opportunities for collaborative projects, you can enhance your students' self-awareness and interpersonal skills. When you implement conflict resolution programs and offer guidance on stress management, you can equip your students with valuable tools for navigating challenges. Remember, you serve as a role model, so focus on demonstrating empathy and emotional regulation in your daily interactions with students.

Every action matters no matter what. It's urgent for educators like you to be more than instructors of content but to act as architects of change. Each strategy discussed is not just a theory; it's a mandate to empower students not just for today but for a future where their impact is not just lasting but transformative. The power to change lives, communities, and the world lies not just in the pages of this book but in you, and in the actions of every educator, the difference makers.

I always end my keynote with the same statement, which is meant to inspire teachers to let them know what an impact they have on their students whether they ever hear it from their students or not, and hopefully it will inspire you to continue to be a difference maker to your students.

Dear teachers, your students may not remember everything you taught them in your class, but they will remember that you cared, showed them grace, made them feel valued, and encouraged them to be their best. They will remember that—and they will remember YOU—forever!

Bibliography

Aliakbari, M., Bozorgmanesh, B., & Gritter, K. (2015). Assertive classroom management strategies and students' performance: The case of EFL classroom. *Cogent Education, 2*(1). DOI: 10.1080/2331186X.2015.1012899

Barbot, B., & Said-Metwaly, S. (2020). Is There Really a Creativity Crisis? A Critical Review and Meta-analytic Re-Appraisal. *Journal of Creative Behavior, 55*(3), 696-709.

Barker G. P., Graham S. (1987). Developmental study of praise and blame as attributional cues. *J. Educ. Psychol.* 79 62 10.1037/0022-0663.79.1.62

Barros, R. M., Silver, E. J., & Stein, R. E. K. (2009). School recess and group classroom behavior. *Pediatrics*, 123(2), 431-436. https://doi.org/10.1542/peds.2007-2825

Blackwell, L. S., Trzesniewski, K. H., & Dweck, C. S. (2007). Implicit theories of intelligence predict achievement across an adolescent transition: a longitudinal study and an intervention. *Child development, 78*(1), 246-263.

Brown, R., & Davis, T. (2020). The Role of Assertiveness in Facilitating Teaching and Learning for EFL Student-Teachers. *TESOL Quarterly, 35*(4), 220-235.

Chang, J. (2011). A Case Study of the "Pygmalion Effect": Teacher Expectations and Student Achievement. *International Education Studies, 4*(1), 198. Retrieved from www.ccsenet. org/ies ISSN 1913-9020 E-ISSN 1913-9039.

Craft, M. (1984). Education for diversity. In *Education and cultural pluralism*, ed. M. Craft, 5–26. London and Philadelphia: Falmer Press.

Davis, K. L., & Montag, C. (2018). Selected Principles of Pankseppian Affective Neuroscience. *Frontiers in Neuroscience, 12,* 1025. https://doi.org/10.3389/fnins.2018.01025

Dweck, C. S. (2006). *Mindset: The New Psychology of Success.* New York, NY: Random House.

Dyer, F. L., & Martin, T. C. (1910). *Edison: His Life and Inventions.* Harper & Brothers.

Erickson, K. I., et al. (2011). Exercise training increases size of hippocampus and improves memory. *Proceedings of the National Academy of Sciences, 108*(7), 3017-3022.

Escalante, J., & Menéndez, R. (Producers), & Nava, R. (Director). (1988). Stand and deliver [Film]. Warner Bros.

Henderlong J., Lepper M. R. (2002). The effects of praise on children's intrinsic motivation: a review and synthesis. *Psychol. Bull.* 128 774–795 10.1037/0033-2909.128.5.774

Hill, L., Williams, J. H., Aucott, L., Thomson, J., & Mon-Williams, M. (2011). How does exercise benefit performance on cognitive tests in primary-school pupils? *Developmental Medicine & Child Neurology, 53*(7), 630-635.

Hillman, C. H., Erickson, K. I., & Kramer, A. F. (2008). Be smart, exercise your heart: exercise effects on brain and cognition. *Nature Reviews Neuroscience, 9*(1), 58-65.

Isaacson, W. (2017). Leonardo da Vinci. Simon & Schuster.

Johnson, A., & Lee, S. (2019). Assertive Classroom Management Strategies: A Key to Effective Teaching and Learning. *Journal of Classroom Management, 10*(2), 75-88.

Johnson, B., & Jones, M. (2021). *Learning on Your Feet: Incorporating Physical Activity into the K–8 Classroom* (2nd ed.). Routledge

Johnson, B., & Johnson, J. (2023). *Becoming a More Assertive Teacher* (1st ed.). Routledge.

Josephson, M. (1959). *Edison: A biography*. New York: McGraw-Hill.

Kim, K. H. (2011). The Creativity Crisis: The Decrease in Creative Thinking Scores on the Torrance Tests of Creative Thinking. *Creativity Research Journal, 23*(4), 285-295.

Land, G., & Jarman, B. (1992). *Breakpoint and beyond: Mastering the future today*. New York: HarperCollins Publishers.

Martin V. Melosi, *Thomas A. Edison and the Modernization of America*, (Glenview, Illinois: Scott, Foresman/Little, Brown Higher Education, 1990) p. 8.

Pontifex, M. B., Saliba, B. J., Raine, L. B., Picchietti, D. L., & Hillman, C. H. (2013). Exercise improves behavioral, neurocognitive, and scholastic performance in children with attention-deficit/hyperactivity disorder. *The Journal of Pediatrics, 162*(3), 543-551.

Raudenbush, S. W. (1984). Magnitude of teacher expectancy effects on pupil IQ as a function of the credibility of expectancy induction: A synthesis of findings from 18 experiments.

Journal of Educational Psychology, 76(1), 85–97. https://doi.org/10.1037/0022-0663.76.1.85

Rosenthal, R., & Jacobson, L. (1968). Pygmalion in the classroom: Teacher expectation and pupils' intellectual development. *The Urban Review, 3*(1), 16-20.

Smith, J. (2018). The Impact of Teacher Assertiveness on Student Performance. *Journal of Educational Psychology, 25*(3), 112-130.

Weiner B. (2011). "An attribution theory of motivation," in *Handbook of Theories of Social Psychology* Vol. 1 eds Van Lange P. A. M., Kruglanski A. W., Higgins E. T. (Thousand Oaks, CA: SAGE;) 135–155

Woolley J.D. (2006). Verbal–behavioral dissociations in development. *Child Dev.* 77 1539–1553 10.1111/j.1467-8624.2006.00956.x

https://www.edutopia.org/article/modeling-assertiveness-students/

https://online.uwa.edu/news/teaching-assertiveness-elementary-students/

https://files.eric.ed.gov/fulltext/EJ1201589.pdf

https://everydayspeech.com/sel-implementation/nurturing assertiveness-in-children-practical-tips-for-elementary-teachers/

https://everydayspeech.com/sel-implementation/promoting-healthy-communication-teaching-assertiveness-in-high-school/

https://soar.suny.edu/handle/20.500.12648/5617

https://www.tandfonline.com/doi/full/10.1080/2331186X.2015.1012899

About the Author

Dr. Brad Johnson is an esteemed educational leader dedicated to transforming the approach of teachers and administrators in schools. With a focus on servant leadership, he emphasizes collaboration and empowering others to maximize their potential. His work is grounded in the belief that effective leadership comes from the heart, fostering positive relationships and leading by example.

With 30 years of experience as a teacher, administrator, and college instructor, Dr. Johnson brings a wealth of knowledge and practical insights to his work. His extensive background in education enables him to connect with educators at all levels and provide strategies that are both impactful and implementable.

Dr. Johnson is the author of 15 influential books on education, including the widely acclaimed *Finding Your Leadership Edge* and the bestseller *Dear Teacher*. His book *Putting Teachers First* is now available in Arabic, further extending his global reach.

Dr. Johnson is renowned for his inspirational and informative presentations, sharing practical strategies and tools with educators worldwide. His keynote speeches, such as "Dear Teacher," address critical issues like self-doubt, imposter syndrome, and fostering a culture of accountability through empowering techniques and strategies.

Ranked #7 in the top 30 Global Gurus in Education, Dr. Johnson's profound impact on the field is recognized internationally. His dynamic presentations inspire and motivate audiences, making him a sought-after speaker at educational conferences and workshops.

To have Dr. Johnson speak at your event, please visit www.doctorbradjohnson.com for more information.

More From TeacherGoals Publishing

Body and Brain Brilliance
By Dr. Lori Desautels

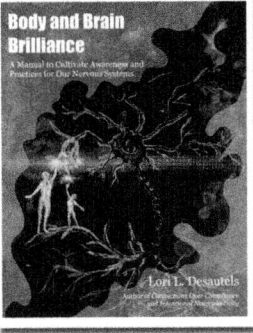

When adults understand their nervous systems, they can identify emotional triggers, detect dysregulation in their bodies and brains, and adapt their responses. This knowledge enables them to approach a dysregulated child with curiosity, compassion, and connection rather than control or escalation.

Body and Brain Brilliance, a neuro-educational guide for all ages, focuses on the science and language of our nervous systems for both educators and students. It explains how our nervous systems store, process, and conserve energy, highlighting the importance of integrating neuroeducational practices in schools. This approach helps to recognize and address the underlying dysregulation and pain in behaviors often mislabeled as aggressive, defiant, or apathetic.

Heartleader
By Matthew Bowerman

Heartleader: (härt-lē-dər) *noun*

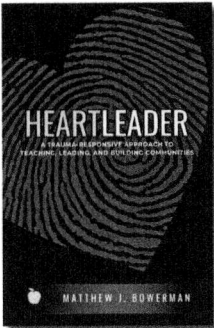

(1) a person who has built a compassionate, empathetic, authentic sense of themselves in order to intentionally love, guide, and empower all aspects of a school community.

(2) a person who believes that love in education is the first and most valuable lesson one can give or receive.

(3) a person who seeks only to lead, live, and learn with love as their guiding syllabus.

From the moment you become part of a school community, it's all about **authentic relationships and authentic love.**

When you lead from the heart, what impact will you create with those you serve?

Heartleader is both an origin story and a trauma-responsive K-12 guide focused on protecting students, supporting staff, and enhancing community ties.

Modern PBL
By Daniel Jones

Dive into the future of education with Daniel Jones's *Modern PBL.* This guide equips educators with strategies to integrate technology and Project-Based Learning (PBL), addressing the challenges presented by AI in classrooms. Key highlights include:

- **Confronting the AI Challenge**
- **Cultivating Authentic Learning**
- **Integrating Technology Seamlessly**
- **Adopting Modern Teaching Practices**
- **Accessing Cutting-Edge Resources**

Daniel Jones, along with insights from global education experts, positions *Modern PBL* as a cornerstone for educators ready to lead in the digital age. This book encourages teachers to embrace and shape the future of education.

Bulk Orders

Need copies for your coworkers or staff? Bulk order your favorite titles and enjoy exclusive discounts. Ask about signed copies and book studies to enhance your reading experience.

Big savings and great learning opportunities await with every bulk purchase!

www.teachergoals.com/bulk

Printed in Great Britain
by Amazon

59590451R00096